SHAW
GEORGE *versus* BERNARD

SHAW

GEORGE *versus* BERNARD

by

J. P. HACKETT

NEW YORK

SHEED & WARD

MCMXXXVII

29766

TO
HELEN

CONTENTS

CONTENTS

PROLOGUE

" When I say that I am an Irishman I mean that I was born in Ireland, and that my native language is the English of Swift and not the unspeakable jargon of the mid-XIX century London newspapers. My extraction is the extraction of most Englishmen : that is, I have no trace in me of the commercially imported North Spanish strain that passes for aboriginal Irish : I am a genuine typical Irishman of the Danish, Norman, Cromwellian, and (of course) Scotch invasions." (*Prefaces by Bernard Shaw*, p. 440.)

OFF the north-west coast of Europe lie two islands. One stretches out, challenging, angular and masculine, from France up into the northern seas. The other rests, demure, compact, feminine, turning an impassive poll to its neighbour and a face full of charm and variety towards the western ocean ; geographically it is staged as a land of withdrawal and mystery, easily exploited by writing men as a place of haunting shadows, melancholy unfulfilment, and vague wearying dreams ; but it was not so from the beginning, a thousand years before the Celtic twilight had dawned in France and England the singing of the Irish poets was full of vitality and a sense of joy and security which triumphs

over time and almost over literal translation into
English :

> Summer has come healthy and free,
> Whence the brown wood is bent to the ground ;
> The slender nimble deer leap,
> And the path of seals is smooth.

> The cuckoo sings gentle music,
> Whence there is smooth peaceful calm ;
> Gentle birds skip upon the hill,
> And swift grey stags.

or again :

> The lowing of heifers in summer,
> Brightest of seasons.
> Not bitter toilsome over the fertile plain,
> Delightful, smooth !

> The voice of the wind against the branchy wood
> Upon the deep blue sky.
> Falls of the river, the note of the swan,
> Delicious music !

It was an attractive spot for poets and for landowners. Over great plains, limestone underground
and soft moisture-laden breezes overhead made
pasture on which cattle fattened visibly from day to
day ; in the broken ground in the hills the grass
grew rich between the rocks and the sheep grew
sleek and thick-coated ; on every hand were brimming rivers and sheltered, fish-laden lakes. To
have ten acres of such land was to be secure, to
have a hundred was to be important, to control
five thousand was to be a great chief. In course of

time landowners and poets combined to devise rules for living and fighting and passing on property. These rules—called the Brehon code—were different from those in operation in the larger island, so different indeed, that their reactions have bewildered the feudal-minded from 1170 to this very day.

There were many visitors to the smaller island even before that date. Scandinavian younger sons were being crowded out at home, and this pleasant resort of natural harbours opening on rich lands drew them strongly. Raids broadened out into invasions and, in the ninth and tenth centuries, the Danish sea-coast settlements were established. Later on more businesslike Norman invasions from Wales were sponsored by English kings, backed by feudal organisation. At first there was fierce opposition, with organised archery beating the battle-axe all along the line, but after a few generations more friendly feelings developed for very natural reasons. The Norman barons studied the Brehon code, and the further they moved inland the fainter became their feudalism. Kings were exacting—hard to please—uncertain ; and in this new country the law for chiefs with a well-armed following was delightful. There were other attractions ; the Irish girls were charming, the salmon fishing marvellous and the hunting simply magnificent. Alliances were made, intermarriages were contracted, and before the Norman conquest was finished the Irishwomen had won.

3

The young de Burghs and Butlers and Fitz-
geralds were running round in homespun kilts
playing native games and chattering Gaelic, and
hearing from their mothers and attendants songs
and stories which stirred curious feelings in their
hearts. In Dublin and its neighbourhood it was
well understood how much the Irish girls were to
blame for the continued failure to establish English
law and order, and in one of the recurrent periods
of resolute government it was resolved that " an
Englishman marrying an Irish wife shall be half
hanged, disembowelled alive, mutilated, and *forfeit
his estate.*"

From about this time—fourteenth century—the
land-lording business in Ireland entered on a new
phase, in which battle-axes and sudden raids figured
less and less, and statutes and lawyers more and
more. Under the new rules the key phrase was,
" he must forfeit his estate." In those days there
were no coal mines—no banks—no Stock Exchange
—no way at all by which a man could live easy
except by owning land. In England every acre
was ear-marked, and into Dublin poured a steady
stream of new English, of land-hungry governors,
attorneys, soldiers of fortune, and men miscel-
laneously on the make.

There were many ways of securing the desired
property, but by far the most effective and permanent was the legal method of finding some property owner guilty of treason, disposing of him in

prison or otherwise, and taking possession of the forfeited estate ; it was usually best to pick on one of the old English who had bagged some good land in the last generation. During the Wars of the Roses, with allegiance divided and fortunes varying, this method was practised in a limited way, but it was a century or more before it could be organised on a sound basis. Then, with the Reformation in progress, with Elizabeth on the warpath, with Fitzgerald, Earl of Desmond, a Catholic, and Butler, Earl of Ormond, a Protestant, and with fanaticism and greed raging together, the new English got their chance at last. They took it eagerly, but the " forfeit-his-estate " axe was now swinging so widely and falling so rapidly that the land market was glutted ; Dublin deputies and their friends could no longer absorb all the territory taken over ; even when Sir Walter Raleigh got 42,000 acres, Edmund Spenser 12,000, and others in proportion, there was still so much to spare that it was peddled in London at twopence an acre. Henceforward the marketing of Irish land became a serious business of state, carried on in a strict and orderly manner with all the weight of English law behind it. Governors continued to feather their nests in a quiet way, but the private enterprise stage was really over. The Plantations were beginning.

The driving forces behind the great Plantation of Ireland—the Cromwellian Hell-or-Connaught

Plantation—came from afar, even from Spain and
Geneva. From 1550 onward a great flood of silver
had poured into Cadiz, and from there into the
currency-hungry cities of Europe as fast as Philip
of Spain could pay for war supplies and ships.
By 1600 the financiers, the manufacturers, and the
traders of Western Europe had the silver and Spain
had the memory of the Armada ; the new middle
class was coming to the fore and getting its first
taste of power.

While the silver was spreading from Spain,
something else less tangible was spreading from
Geneva. Jean Calvin, with his genius for precision and organisation, was forging a new creed
and a new code, offering sanctity and certainty to
pious Protestants dazed by Lutheran somersaults.
It offered also two attractive by-products—self-
righteousness and a perfectly disciplined militia—
to the new middle class. The burgesses loved the
new code, with its exact prescription of conduct
and even of dress, its insistence on honesty, thrift
and unceasing devotion to business in all waking
hours of all working days, and its rule that savings
must not be spent light-heartedly on fine arts,
games and general jollification, but turned back
into development and increased production. They
reached out on all sides, buying and controlling
greater and wider interests, till, in Holland and
France, Calvinistic organisations were strong as
Fascist States.

In England—bound closely to Holland in Elizabeth's time—the tides of silver and Calvinism rose together. Royalty, on a fixed income, was desperately hard up ; between 1570 and 1648 prices trebled, and Charles I, facing the steepest part of the rise, found himself also facing the grim task of making ends meet by taxing the new-rich Puritans. They didn't like it : they were making money hand over fist on a rising market ; they commanded the services of men and their sense of power was growing ; they hadn't a cent to spare for anything but goods . . . besides, was it not sinful to contribute to the support of a cavalier court and a state church almost popish ?

The royal exchequer was in a parlous condition when some genius hit on a plan for replenishing it and at the same time fulfilling so many other purposes that its wizardry makes the head reel. The most dazzling Wall Street coups are bungling crudities compared with this great scheme for selling Ireland : it promised to yield over a million pounds—to wipe out the King's enemies—to settle the Irish problem—and above all to give the rich merchants of the towns a promising lock-up security with prospects of capital appreciation, or alternatively to provide them with enough fertile Irish soil to make them landed gentry in a country where their humble forbears were unknown ; and it did not cost the vendors a penny.

The plan was absolutely legal. It was called

"Charles I, An. 16, Chap. XXXIII, A.D. 1640—
An Act for the speedy and effectuall reducing of
the Rebells in his Majestie's Kingdom of Ireland
to their due obedience to his Majestie and the
Crowne of England," and it provided for the sale
of 2,500,000 acres of Irish land in small lots at
about ten shillings an acre freehold.

The money so raised was to be used to finance
an armed expedition into Ireland. The General
and officers were to be nominated and controlled
by a committee representing the subscribers and
members of Parliament.

The scheme worked and the money rolled in :

John Pim, Esq., a member of ye House	£600
Oliver Cromwell, Esq., a member of ye House	£300
Thomas Pargiter, grocer . . .	£100
Thomas Viner, of London, goldsmith	£200
Isaacke Jurin, of London, weaver .	£100
Richard Wade, of London, carpenter	£6,100

and so on by hundreds and thousands. But curiously enough—and this is where the New Yorker
takes off his hat to the Englishman—the private
army, when equipped, instead of going to fight the
King's enemies in Ireland, turned into an English
rebel army, fighting Charles at Edgehill. That was
in 1642. It was 1649 before Cromwell was able to
dispose of the King, but the subscribers and their
parliamentary backers had not lost sight of the main

8

issue, and immediately after the execution he was sent off to quell the Irish and secure the land for the bondholders.

The Cromwellian invasion opened strongly at Drogheda, and in a short time the English Republic had command of all strategic points, and it only remained to clear the existing population from their farms and estates. Far more than 2,500,000 acres were now required, for Commonwealth funds were exhausted, and it had been decided to pay the soldiers in debentures, backed by good, rich Irish soil. The clearing was a problem. If the property-owning population had been all Irish, it would have been simple enough ; or even if they had been mixed Irish and English and all Catholic, it would have been easy to devise some religious test which would oust them ; but they were mixed Irish-English-Catholic-Protestant, and there was nothing for it but to hold the fortified centres and starve them off. So on July 1st, 1651, the Commissioners of Ireland were found securing special supplies for the Army— " swords, pikes, powder horns . . . scythes, sickles, reaphooks, whetstones, rubstones . . . and Bibles." They were just in time for that year's harvest. The crops were cut down before they ripened, and by 1652 organised famine was in full swing and the landholders were beginning to disappear.

But the process of starvation was too slow, and in 1653 the Commissioners had to try and rush things by making an order that all those who could

9

not secure from a court of Cromwellian judges set
up at Athlone a decree of " Constant good affection
to the Commonwealth " must transplant themselves
to Connaught. This was effective—it ruled out all
Irish and nearly all English owners—for even the
most far-seeing Protestants had been inclined to
back the King.

The importation of Bibles for the army of occupation seems curious till it becomes clear that Ireland
was looked on as the Promised Land, and the Bible
as a charter from heaven plus title-deeds. (Arch-
bishop Ussher was still living ; he had fixed the
date of Creation at 4004 B.C., and any Cromwellian
who didn't believe that was excommunicated, *i.e.*,
he got no land.) The Commissioners who had been
charged under the Act of 1640 to distribute land
were of the elect. A record of the times (dated
November 9th, 1653) describes them as " overwhelmed with a sense of their difficulties and of
their own unworthiness for so great a service . . .
they therefore fasted and enjoined the same thing
on all Christian friends in Ireland, and invited the
commanders and officers of the army to join them
in lifting up prayers with strong crying and tears
to Him to whom nothing is too hard, that His
servants whom He had called forth in this day to
act in their great transactions might be made
faithful and carried on by His own outstretched
arm against all opposition and difficulty to do what
was pleasing in His sight," and later, on May 31st,

1654, they write : " We are somewhat in a confused posture yet, with our transplantation, many are gone but many others play ' loath to depart.' And many are dispensed with, as particularly one whole town, Cashel, towards which we had no great obligation upon us. But the Lord who is a jealous God, and more knowing of, as well as jealous against, their iniquity than we are, by a fire on 23rd inst. hath burned down the whole town in a little more than a quarter of an hour, except some few houses that a few English lived in, which were wonderfully preserved, being in the midst of the town, and the houses round each burnt to the ground, yet *they* preserved."

About the same time the officers of Dublin, Carlow, Wexford and Kilkenny wrote to the Lord Deputy—" the first purpose of transplantation is to prevent those of natural principles becoming one with these Irish as well in affinity as idolatry as many thousands did who came over in Queen Elizabeth's time, many of which have had a deep hand in all the late murders and massacres. And shall we join in affinity with the people of these abominations ? Would not the Lord be angry with us till he consumes us, having said, ' The land which you go to possess is an unclean land, because of the filthiness of the people that dwell therein. Ye shall not give your sons to their daughters, nor take their daughters to your sons,' as it is in Ezra ix. 11, 12, 14. ' Nay, ye shall surely root them out

before you lest they cause you to forsake the Lord
your God ' (Deut. vii. 23, 4, 16)."

The officers got their way, and young William
Spenser, grandson of Edmund, and all the rest
had to get out to Connaught or elsewhere to make
room for the cavalrymen. Among them was a
Colonel Ponsonby.

Such was the Cromwellian invasion. While the
officers were bargaining over their booty, young
William Shaw was learning to ride a horse in Hampshire, practising sword-play, reading his Bible and
otherwise preparing for his trip to Ireland. He came
into action in 1690 at the Battle of the Boyne,
where Ponsonby-Shaw cavalry helped to establish
the other William on the throne of England and
incidentally bind the Shaws and Ponsonbys in
enduring friendship when they settled down, safe
under the Protestant succession, in that lovely
estate in south Kilkenny, where the soft-turfed
lands slope down so gently to the deep-flowing
River Suir.

[*Note.*—The above account of the Great Plantation has been summarised from Prendergast's
Cromwellian Settlement of Ireland, which is a careful
account of the facts with references to all original
documents.]

CHAPTER I

In 1878 a young man of twenty-two, with a capital of sixpence invested in cheap white paper, began to write. By 1890 he was sending out screeches with his pen which were echoing through London and aggravating everyone. By 1900 he was pouring out plays of a peculiar, intimate, effervescent quality which drew large audiences and made them laugh in a strange, uneasy way. By 1910 the spending public had decided that though he was a very curious fellow and though no one could possibly agree with him about Socialism and all that, he must be quite respectable, because he was making money without being put in jail. Soon, the plain white paper with the fine neat writing was fluttering round the world—magically turning into thousands and thousands of crisp clean banknotes.

To-day there is no man alive more certain of an audience. He has the front page of the world's Press freely at his disposal and he can go anywhere and fill a hall to the brim at a moment's notice with spectators and listeners, eager to see him and hear him mocking them and their ways of living in a clear, mellow, pleasant voice. He does not get publicity, he *is* publicity. Half a century ago people

13

found him and his opinions unbearable. Thirty years ago earnest young men eager for the limelight tried omniscience and inconoclasm—thinking they were using his methods—and wondered at the lack of results. Just before the war his fame as a great jester was growing steadily, though some occasionally tried to flick him away with a phrase as though he were a troublesome insect. During the war he was in disgrace with the public, but after it he rose into general favour like a rocket. The chocolate soldier was no longer a joke, and it was found that many of his jests had been earnest. He was labelled " prophet," and his views began to be accepted as recklessly as they had been rejected in pre-war times. To-day, he is pointed to proudly by Britons who believe he is English, as the greatest living dramatist, and claimed eagerly by others who think he is Irish, as a sample of the genius which sprouts so readily on their native soil. He is accepted as a great man who is in some special way different from other men. It is not that he is a great dramatist, or a great speaker, or a great Socialist, or a great critic, or even that he is a combination of all four. A man could be all these and yet miss that capacity to arouse curiosity and expectancy in all classes on a world-wide scale which is George Bernard Shaw's special prerogative.

In some mysterious way he provokes people he has never seen to write books about him. They want to tell the world what a great man he is, or that he is not such a great man, or how he inspired them, or how they discovered him. *The* book is, of course, the authorised biography by Archibald Henderson, an American professor of mathematics. It is a model of industry, a meticulous record of Shaw's progress on every field, with a wealth of annotation ; it is a most carefully written volume, indispensable for reference, but it tells far more about the author than about his subject. Other commentaries, with one exception, have the same mirror-like quality. They vary in key from Henderson's ecstatic tome to the offensive and defensive work by Frank Harris ; but when they have finished, the picture of Shaw is stiff and patchy, and the human qualities of the writer pulse through every chapter, particularly in those places where he describes how he corrected, or advised, or disagreed with his hero, with the excited and triumphant air of the child at the Zoo telling how he slapped the elephant. Harris was up in arms all the time : " Our chief difference is that Shaw wanted to be a man of action while I actually was." . . . " So he isn't as great as he himself supposes." He went on like that till it was almost pathetic. Only once did he provoke his subject to retort ; Shaw was like Harris, and most other men, on one point : he could not stand being called a prude, and was prepared to go to great lengths to show that the epithet was undeserved.

The study of Shaw written by Chesterton in 1905

was the exception. Its insight was uncanny, even if he did write like a Newfoundland dog pretending to be a kitten. It is impossible not to have sympathy with that exasperated reader who printed " beautifully written bunkum " on the title page of the copy of Chesterton's *Shaw* which still circulates in a Dublin library ; so it must have seemed to thousands, but the bunkum has turned out to be an appreciation of Shaw as a sincere thinker and a great dramatist, in days when opinion was divided between " brazen thruster " and " gifted clown " ; and the penetrating analysis of the man and his outlook with which it ends continues to-day to attest the soundness of the criticism and the consistency of the outlook. It was, of course, impossible for Chesterton to do justice to Shaw ; his mountainous generosity of spirit and his absurd English tolerance stood in his way at every turn ; here where weakness showed, the chance of a fine malicious twist of phrase was missed, and there where impish glee over individual inconsistency was called for, there was nothing but outrageous laughter at the way men are bound together in universal frailty. Fair and free as is this study of Shaw, it does not do anything to solve the mystery of the quality which induces Englishmen, Russians, Americans, Japanese, and Germans, to offer common worship at the shrine of Shaw and to pour gold into his lap. Like other mysteries of the kind, like Chaplin's charming twisted smile and Shake-

speare's word-music, it is without formula and its
effects cannot be communicated at second-hand
any more than the manner of it can be successfully
used by imitators. It must be tasted at the source.
Those who wish to know about Shaw must read
Shaw; and even those who can't stand him should
read him for the exhilaration of thinking of the
things they would like to do to him. He caters for
all tastes. Politicians and diplomats will find him
full of meat. Preachers who feel themselves getting
stale will rise from his writings with words trembling
on their lips. Mothers will find his phrases excellent material with which to quell rebellious
daughters, and rebellious daughters will find him
their best backer. Burglars will follow him with
zest tempered with horror at his views on private
property. Murderers will want to get back to
work when they find him coming their way :

> If I had the opportunity of conversing with
> the ghost of an executed murderer, I have no
> doubt he would begin to tell me eagerly about
> his trial, with the names of the distinguished
> ladies and gentlemen who honoured him with
> their presence on that occasion, and then about
> his execution. All of which would bore me
> exceedingly. I should say, "My dear sir :
> such manufactured ceremonies do not interest
> me in the least. I know how a man is tried,
> and how he is hanged. I should have had you
> killed in a much less disgusting, hypocritical,

and unfriendly manner if the matter had been in my hands. What I want to know about is the murder. How did you feel when you committed it? Why did you do it? What did you say to yourself about it? If, like most murderers, you had not been hanged, would you have committed other murders? Did you really dislike the victim, or did you want his money, or did you murder a person whom you did not dislike, and from whose death you had nothing to gain, merely for the sake of murdering? If so, can you describe the charm to me? Does it come upon you periodically; or is it chronic? Has curiosity anything to do with it?" I would ply him with all manner of questions to find out what murder is really like; and I should not be satisfied until I had realised that I, too, might commit a murder, or else that there is some specific quality present in a murderer and lacking in me. And, if so, what that quality is. (*Prefaces*, p. 113.)

Funny, isn't it? It looks like sheer light-hearted, inconsequent, comic writing. It is difficult to believe that he was intensely in earnest, and bent only on making his case in the most pungent possible way for the particular method of dramatic presentation with which he was concerned at the moment he was writing.

The person who is curious about Shaw—and who

18

can fail to be curious about a man who, early in his teens, decided to be honest with himself about himself and about the world as he saw it, and was able to keep it up in private for nearly seventy years, and in public for half a century without being massacred ?—the person who is curious about Shaw must study him in the original. He may hate his assurance and damn his impudence, but he will not be able to deny his steadfastness of purpose and heroic honesty of thought and expression, however much he may dislike the creed which has the writer in its grip.

In days to come, when Universities become less like highly exclusive clubs with labelled rooms and channelled ritual, someone may be inspired to suggest the award of a G.B.S. degree for students who take an interest in living men and women rather than in extracts of literature or preserved science. With the half hundredweight, or so, of Shaw's published writings to start with, it should be easy to organise the course of studies. Set lectures would be prohibited, and a candidate for the degree would have to spend half his time in and about libraries, classrooms and common-rooms, as the fancy moved him, and the other half at municipal council meetings, trade union gatherings, plays, concerts, churches, hospitals, factories, business men's lunch-rooms, and so on ; for at least one month he would have to work as temporary clerk in a Civil Service office. He would be required after

three years to show that he had a first-hand knowledge of Shaw's views and of the activities of those
places he had seen ; and he would then be turned
loose and at any subsequent date—up to fifty years
later—he would receive the G.B.S. degree if he
were able to :

(1) Give a clear statement of his belief.

(2) Give a clear description of his normal daily
behaviour.

(3) Show that there was some reasonable connection between (1) and (2).

It would do Universities no end of good to get off
the beaten track. They cannot go on for ever with
their compartmented classics and history from
authorised text-books ; or can they? At any
rate, here at their hand is a man who has tried
a great practical experiment with himself, and
got mixed up with the affairs which will be history
in a hundred years' time, and who has most carefully and accurately recorded his observations and
conclusions. He is as usable in his own way as a
high-power microscope or explosive, and the process
which goes on in his pages is as exciting as a steeple-
chase. Unofficially and outside institutional walls
he has been in use as a handbook, a moral support,
a warning, an excuse, a stimulus, a guide. He is a
wonderful educator with the great and unusual
value that he has nothing *specific* to teach ; nothing
seems to irritate him more than to be told by his
disciples that they are doing or thinking just what

he says, or that they have fixed up their domestic
affairs in accordance with his precepts. They miss
his main point when they take over one of his sentences and bury themselves alive in it. His formula
has always been that formulation for others is not
only impertinent but impossible, and if people are
silly enough to swallow any of his prescriptions
without criticism, they can only blame themselves for the results. Accordingly, he pursues his
prophetic way like one of those modern high-speed
grindstones, guaranteed to knock some sparks out
of the hardest material. He ranges widely enough
to offer every man a test bench, where he can sit
down with his thought in its crude state and grind
his opinions into usable shape by holding them up
against this impossible high-velocity Shaw. Re-
moval of all loose parts and soft spots is guaranteed.

The range of his researches and the varying play
of his interests are irritating at first. People don't
like being switched from religion to Blackpool,
thence to suicide, back to plays and books, out to
Florence Nightingale and away to the South Pole
while reading half a page of printed matter (*Prefaces*, p. 341). They like a man who sticks to his
last, and these flickering changes bewilder them as
the sudden and incomprehensible changes on the
screen bewilder the stranger who enters a cinema
after the show has started. If he has the patience
to wait and sit through the picture again, bewilderment will vanish and the jerks which formerly

annoyed may delight him ; but who is going back
to 1856 (or 1690) to sit through Shaw ? It is easier
to scold him patronisingly for not settling down to
be a straight dramatist, or to regret that a man
with his splendid knowledge of psychology, or
medical practice, or phonetics, or housing, or diplo-
macy, does not enrich the world by spending his
whole time in one of these fields instead of dropping
a bomb into it as he flies past. Still his admirers
could put up with his respect for their omnivorous-
ness if he stopped there and conformed to their
wish that he should occupy a particular kind of
pedestal in each field of activity. His failure to
satisfy them in this way is his chief offence. They
are serious-minded people, and they know and feel
the intensity of his seriousness about those things
in which they are interested, but they simply cannot
stand the inconsequence which is always lurking
behind his great moments. Or, rather, they suspect
and fear its presence ; and they earnestly long to
remake him in their own image and likeness, and
continually appeal to him in agonised tones not
to spoil his noblest efforts with irreverent and
irresponsible anti-climax.

One of them, Mr. Collis, after showing his hand
with the gambit, " When I was a jellyfish I thought
as a jellyfish, but now that I am a man I think
as a man," and offering incense in the approved
manner, goes on to chide, reprove, and scold his
hero for his inconsistency and his bedevilment of

22

his choicest work. He at first complains of the incompatibility of *Man and Superman* with *Back to Methuselah*, but he has not much justification here, for never did one work grow more logically out of another than the play of 1921 out of the philosophy of 1902. Later, however, he makes home thrusts : he finds something curious in the last act of *Major Barbara*, when Shaw, by a sudden leap into farce, " seems to do his utmost to prevent the audience, or an impatient reader, from following Undershaft's extremely difficult line of argument ; " he is just as sound when he revolts against the anticlimax to the shooting of Napoleon, in *Back to Methuselah*, and accuses Shaw of sinking into " low comedy and vulgar farce ; " and he is in a majority of a million when he writhes at the *St. John* epilogue. But then, when he is on the trail of something really interesting, when he is a man holding in his hand three interlocking clues to the solution of his mystification, he drops them and turns jellyfish with : " Whenever we are allowed to lose ourselves in some particularly fine passage we are always in danger of being rudely jerked back to earth by some paltry joke," and again with : " Why these comic kicks ? . . . They ravage their way into the loftiest passages, laying waste the exalted theme." The worshippers want their Shaw cut up into uniform lengths and laid out on a slab, but he refuses to be embalmed. In truth, he is alive and kicking, and some of the " comic kicks " are far more worthy

23

of careful examination than the ballyhoo passages which any literary hack can turn out with a little practice. His disciples sigh and feel that these paltry jokes are mistakes, instead of facts which must be reckoned with in any serious consideration of Shaw. The history of science is littered with just such " mistakes "—facts that will not fit a pet theory, or clash with some cramped assumption absorbed as final truth at the age of ten and made the bedrock of the beliefs of a lifetime. Sometimes it looks as though a motherly Nature scattered abnormalities around, knowing that man was so full of himself he would never notice anything till he barked his shins on it. And then instead of being grateful he grumbles and mutters about " Nature's mistakes." Uranus was supposed to be misbehaving himself as a planet till someone had the sense to see that the " mistakes " were his frantic efforts to introduce Neptune. Radium tried again and again to attract men's attention by outraging all elemental conventions. Bernard Shaw, obviously at heart a dear, sensitive, charitable gentleman, behaves like a word-fed rotary machine-gun, and instead of getting the attention such a phenomenon deserves, he is greeted—first with shouts of Ruffian ! Scoundrel !—then with roars of laughter—and finally with rounds of applause, mixed with the scoldings of those who have looked into the depths of his mind and longed to put it to rights.

These are the comments of men. Women have not said so much about him, but what they do say is very much to the point. Three gifted women have summed him up in a single word, and each of the words is worth noting. Mrs. Patrick Campbell, rejoicing in early memories of the circus, gave him one look and said, " Joey." Mrs. Beatrice Webb, gathering her Shaw statistics together in one careful syllable, labelled him " Sprite." And Ellen Terry, with insight passing all analysis, went straight to the heart of the matter and called him " Bernie."

Why all this contradiction and mystery? It can't be helped; that's how all good stories begin, and the Shaw story is one of the best. He has told it all in his writings, but it is a difficult story to follow, partly because it is a long story, partly because he has tried to force the whole truth into a home-made creed, and partly because even the best of trumpets cannot blow itself effectively. The key to the story is his creed and the vigour with which he practises it. For he *has* a definite belief about the world and his place in it, and he *lives* his belief. He doesn't merely live up to it or turn to it on special occasions with a shamefaced awkwardness or keep it in the background as a fire-escape ; he fills his life with it, in fact the core of it is that his creed and his life are as nearly one as he can make them. The creed is odd, but there is no doubt about the sincerity of his faith or the works with which he backs it ; mountains have been moved, and even shaken till their rocks rattled, by the grip and impact of the ideas spread on that plain white paper in such fine neat writing. He has never tried to conceal this creed, and never wavered from it. From the *Quintessence of Ibsenism*, in 1890, to the preface to *Back to Methuselah*, in 1921, and on to the *Black Girl*, in 1932, he has continued to describe it and preach it in general and particular terms, in fact he has really never done anything else but write about it and its ramifications. For the sake of knowing what Shaw is driving at, and understanding those things which puzzle his admirers and even himself, it is worth while taking a good square look at this Life Force religion of his, and tracing it to its source. Impertinence ? Nonsense ! Religion may be a private affair in some cases, but the Life Force religion, which Shaw has preached around the world, and which is breaking out in such curious forms in Europe at present, is everybody's business.

CHAPTER II

THIS is the story of Shaw's creed as it looks from
the outside. It is set out here because it is by far
the most important thing about him. It is the
key to his conduct. The case to be made is—that a
man who had a real belief in the tale of creation to
be told in this chapter, and accepted the logical consequences of that belief, would behave as Shaw
behaves ; and there is also the stranger case to be
made—that a man driven by an intense love for
truth, and a great respect for facts, to be dubious
about the tale, would also behave as Shaw behaves.
He would be a master of anti-climax. This is all
very mysterious, and it is right that it should be so,
for at the back of it all is a real mystery—the
mystery of being human—in which you and I and
Shaw are all equally concerned, and for which let
it be freely admitted no explanation is offered.
All that is offered is a sorting out of the facts in
the hope that some enlightenment will follow.
Now this sorting out, particularly when it concerns
itself with another man's creed, is far from being a
simple matter. It is essential that the creed be
stated accurately and at the same time in such a
way that one can have sympathy with Shaw's

championship of it ; the reader must both understand it and see it somewhat as Shaw sees it, otherwise the promised key will be missing ; but he must
first be warned of two difficulties which crop up
at this point.

The first is the obvious difficulty of prejudice
which always arises when an outsider is stating the
creed of an insider. Even when the outsider is
trying to be a Christian, he is just as liable to error
as the next man. The zoologist impaling butterflies
in a case, even with the best will in the world, is
liable to bruise something ; if he is a very expert
zoologist with a pet theory, he is sure to make a
special collection of butterflies to tally with it ; in
his regard for scientific truth he may even snip the
wings from any butterfly which dares to conflict
with his theory, or twist some poor creature into
an unnatural shape to demonstrate his ingenuity.
The history of science is as deeply littered as the
history of religion with cases of the strange behaviour
of men who, above all things, wanted their own way.
The outsider usually wants to discredit the creed
which conflicts with his own, and it will always
be found that his tendency to distort truth is
directly proportional to the weakness of his own
position. Shaw, for instance, tries to make a place
for his own doctrine by suggesting that Christians
believe :

that the world was made in the year 4004 B.C. ;
that damnation means an eternity of blazing

28

brimstone ; that the Immaculate Conception
means that sex is sinful and that Christ was
parthenogenetically brought forth by a virgin
descended in like manner from a line of virgins
right back to Eve ; that the Trinity is an anthro-
pomorphic monster with three heads which
are yet only one head ; that in Rome the bread
and wine on the altar become flesh and blood,
and in England, in a still more mystical manner,
they do and they do not ; that the Bible is an
infallible scientific manual, an accurate his-
torical chronicle and a complete guide to
conduct ; that we may lie and cheat and
murder and then wash ourselves innocent in
the blood of the lamb on Sunday at the cost
of a *credo* and a penny in the plate, and so on
and so forth.

And then goes on to make his real point :

Civilisation cannot be saved by people not
only crude enough to believe these things, but
irreligious enough to believe that such a belief
constitutes a religion. The education of children cannot safely be left in their hands. If
dwindling sects like the Church of England,
the Church of Rome, the Greek Church, and
the rest, persist in trying to cramp the human
mind within the limits of these grotesque per-
versions of natural truths and poetic meta-
phors, then they must be ruthlessly banished
from the schools until they either perish in

general contempt, or discover the soul that is hidden in every dogma. (*Prefaces*, p. 517.)
This illustrates the difficulty perfectly. When so scrupulous and fair-minded a professional prophet cannot keep straight in dealing with a creed alien to his own, it is well for the amateur to be wary lest he, too, only succeed in adding to the sum of human ignorance and confusion. The process of skinning the believer—of separating him from that which is part of himself—must be preceded by study and undertaken with caution, if anything more than a few valueless mutilated scraps of his belief are to be secured.

The second difficulty is that creeds have gone out of fashion and that words like " belief " and " faith " are losing their meaning. So many certainties have been disturbed of late that people are beginning to put their trust in the belief that belief is not to be trusted. It is hard to make clear the significance of a real creed to those who are turning their believing faculty inside out and using it to doubt with. It is easy enough to describe Shaw's creed, or at least to set out the basis of it, but it is necessary also to show something of what it means to him, to convey some impression of the intensity with which he holds it. Many men have views on evolution, and the Life Force, similar to Shaw's, but they do not make them a personal matter ; they believe *about* evolution, he believes *in* it ; they think it is something which happened millions of years ago and has nothing to do with them; he thinks it is something which is happening to-day and has everything to do with him, that it is him, and he is it, and that together they are life. But perhaps this is not making matters any easier and it may be better to seek some common ground to show what is here meant by belief.

Take the Derby at Epsom. Even in the upper reaches of the Amazon and the inner recesses of China, the English Derby is common property; every man knows that it is a race for the best three-year-olds in the world, or if he doesn't, tries to pretend that he does. He is ashamed, and rightly ashamed, of not knowing such a splendid and reputable fact. There is simply no doubt about the Derby. Some people have more intimate knowledge than others, and can say off-hand that Wragg won on Blenheim in 1930, others think that a Derby winner should have a good chance in the Grand National; but these little contrasts only help us to enjoy our certainty; they don't alter the fact or our belief about it, or our readiness to get together over it. On the contrary those who are strangers to Epsom and know but little are always anxious to be put in touch with those who know something, and those who have information are always delighted to share it abroad. Here is genuine belief. The creed, if you like, is primitive, and has but one article, but see how the belief remains equally certain through all degrees of intensity and how

minor misconceptions have no effect either on the
reality of the event or the validity of belief in it.
But, some may object, this state of certainty is not
belief at all but mere knowledge based on direct
experience, such as science gives. They would
have more than a little difficulty in applying this
objection to the Australian who always backs the
favourite, or to the enthusiast, born in 1887, who
believes that Hermit won in grand style in 1867.
And even if the sceptic could prove his point and
show that the mundane belief that there is such a
race as the Derby is not a belief at all, he would
still have to face the task of demolishing the other
deeper belief connected with this race. It is a
wonderful belief which has nothing to do with
the restricted realm of science. Behind the fact,
behind the event, is a faith which transcends
experience and which, in a sense, precedes and
materialises the event. The sceptic, if he is ignorant
of horse-racing, will unfortunately not see this ;
to him the whole affair may even seem a sordid
matter of money and horses. He will not see that
a belief in something quite intangible is at work
behind the scenes, brushing aside doubt, triumphing
over a million difficulties, bringing men of all
parties together, and making them at home with
one another. Men, for a little while, have a real
belief in honour. The Derby is what it is because
so many people want to see and share in an honest
race, and because they believe that here at least the

SHAW

men are giving the horses a chance. Out of this
spontaneous act of belief is born the glory of that
day at Epsom.

Now there are some people who believe that this
race takes place, but who never saw it and would
not cross the road to see it ; this belief is to them
only a belief *about* the Derby, it is a seed perishing
annually on stony soil. But consider the others :
think of the man who loves horses and the simmering life of great crowds ; who has never missed
that Epsom meeting since he was a boy ; who
looks forward to it from year to year ; who talks,
reads, dreams and lives in a horse world " of risk
and trust and speculation and daring ; " whose
highest ambition is to breed, own, train, and lead
in a Derby winner. He believes *in* the Derby and
partakes of it in a way which no mere half-crown-
each-way partaker understands ; he is no more
certain than anyone else that the event is real and
will recur annually, but the quality of his belief
is different and is not to be conveyed by any word
picture of the crowds, the horses and the race,
however accurate and detailed. It is a real
belief.

Real beliefs, strangely enough, are not a guarantee
of the truth of what is believed ; they seem to wind
themselves about fictions and myths as easily as
about facts and truth, but their effect is always the
same : " They create, as the case may be, heroes
and saints, great leaders, statesmen, preachers and

S. 33 D

reformers, the pioneers in discovery in science, visionaries, fanatics, knight-errants, demagogues and adventurers," and also, Newman might have added, great racing men and great dramatists. But whatever the type, the first step towards knowing the man is to discover the outlines of his creed.

The creed of the Life Force as outlined by Shaw has scarcely any outlines. His version of Creative Evolution is somewhat different from Bergson's whose particular speciality it is. They seem to have arrived at certain similar points of view independently, and each has brought them to a focus in his own way. Shaw was first in the field, with a multitude of facts and instances, launching his campaign for the new religion, in concrete form, from every angle of human interest. Bergson came later, with close-knit argument and his ingenious idea about time, and more cautiously put very much the same story into abstract form. He began with a goddess called *la durée*, threw in one of those strange philosophic gods called " an infinity of shooting out " and made them jointly responsible for everything, literally every thing. It is all very ingenious. *La durée* in particular is a fascinating creature, but she does not appear in Shaw's version of Creative Evolution, nor does he seem to realise how necessary she is, nor the difficulties which evolutionary theories get into when their authors neglect to put some curb on the *time* which they lose so recklessly to produce man

34

and the amœba. Bergson knew all about that ; but Shaw was shy of abstract thought, he liked real things—real people—real happenings—on every page, and he left *time* to look after itself.

The idea of Creative Evolution is based, in the first place, on the facts put forward, from time to time, in favour of the theory of the gradual evolution of species. It is not concerned with, or, at best, only gives a chilly nod to, other facts having to do with the gradual evolution of the whole universe. Its date of emergence is about 1859, when *The Origin of Species* was published by Charles Darwin, and when for the first time the theory of evolution was dealt with in a thorough and scientific manner. There had been plenty of isolated, half-hearted attempts to launch evolutionary theories in former years and centuries, but this was the first thoughtful, well-planned, comprehensive attempt. Darwin was a scientist of the old school. He said in effect : " Here's what happens and here's why it happens," and left it open to anyone to check both statements. He was certainly elated by the all-round neatness of his theory, and the way all his facts fitted in, but he never lost his head about it. He knew that whatever success he had gained in explaining " How is a hen ? " he was as far off as ever from the answer to " Why is a hen ? " Intrepid admirers found no difficulty about such questions, and, sheltered behind the reputations of real scientists, they started off to produce the first scientific journ-

alism—all about molecules and mammals and the
sheer inevitability of everything. Between the
straight science of Darwin and this popular science,
there slowly developed other growths fostered by
those who wished to save something of value from
the mechanists and hammer the new hypothesis
into a religion.

One of these growths was inspired, taken in hand,
nourished, trimmed and tended by a succession of
men—Butler, Ibsen, Wells for awhile, Bergson and
the rest—so that it grew and grew like Jack's
beanstalk. But the fairy story is upside down, the
hero is up in the topmost branch, playing solitaire,
and the ogre is down below tangled in the roots.

To find these roots go back five thousand years
—and then a million years—and then back over
æons and eras—back and back till you are dazed
and floundering in the mists of time, and can
imagine dimly only one formless meaningless Thing
which is not time or space, but is somehow entangled
in them, which has no parts but only potentiality,
which has no quality whatever, but is itself meaningless unceasing Action. This Thing is the Ultimate Mystery, the meaning of all things reduced
to the very lowest term. It cannot be described,
but can be pictured dimly, in those far-off stretches
of time, from the results of its experiments, as " a
seething omnipotent unordered force "—" a whirling
vortex of meaningless energy "—" an infinity of
aimless shooting out." Blend with this first shadowy

impressionistic glimpse of origins an idea of terrific
striving power ; there must be no values, no evil,
no good, nothing except infinite, restless Power ;
but do not confuse this Power with the mechanical
power then being born in the first cataclysmic
delivery of flying particles which were to be atoms,
nor yet identify it with the vital power which
appeared later on this earth, as the basic force
surged wildly in the atoms it had created by chance.
This basic Force lies behind, and is the unwitting
cause of those minor powers ; it is not apart from
them, but, blindly asserting itself, is embedded and
enwrapped in its own assertions.

So the first tiny cell, trembling into life on this
planet, was just a chance experiment which neither
knew, nor was known by, the Life Force. Neither
it nor its successors knew, as they rose into life and
motion with time and faded away into death, that
they did so but to maintain this blind experimenting
Force which pushed this way and that ; sometimes
failing and coming to a full stop, but always thrust-
ing out in new directions, moving along other
branches, up and up and up ; undying, as it passed
from parent to child, and spurred, through its
sensitive appetites, each fresh dwelling to build up
the new habits, which were to become new functions, in the budding cells of fresh generations. So,
in the beginning of the era of living things, confusion reigned, as the surviving inventions battled
with new creations, as the old experiments of

Floods and Frosts, so successful in the formative ages, wiped out the new ones of Plants and Animals, and as great Beasts preyed on one another, driven by the blind Force which surged within them, and emerged as the Will-to-Live. Here is no chance mechanism, but a positive Vital Force " willing " the things which help it to survive. The herbage-cropping quadruped, starving in drought, is driven by some inner urge to satisfy his hunger with foliage which his ancestors ignored, and so survives in conditions which destroyed them. Centuries later, a descendant, finding the foliage beyond his reach, uses the same will-to-live and purposefully up-stretches with all his might to reach the higher branches. He and his offspring may perish, but, sooner or later in the line, the neck-producing cells co-ordinate under the creating impulse, passed down from the pioneer, and the long-necked giraffe is born.

Thus Life moves on trying—willing—learning in its several units, till at last by many striving coinci-dences self-consciousness, reason and imagination blend, and man emerges. For thousands of years he too stumbles on, carrying with him traces of the spent forces of other ages at war with these newer and nobler efforts of the Life Force ; lower instincts from the past fight wildly against the uplifting thoughts of the present ; from time to time the Life Force produces outstanding men, to whom some idea is all-in-all, who give themselves

to it unstintingly, and in so doing "create."
Towards the end of the nineteenth century, some
such men—hitherto acting blindly—become dimly
conscious of a Great Purpose. Here and there
through Europe and America appear individuals
who realise that the race is greater than the person,
and that it is being held back in its upward struggle
by those who cling in blind, static superstition to
outworn creeds, fixed standards, and tribal ritual.
These New Men, in their consciousness of the
upward and onward thrust of evolution and of the
part they are called on to play, are the true heirs
of the ages. They are akin to the artist-prophets of
former years, but with a difference. They know
that they are sports. They know vaguely the meaning of themselves. They know that they are the very
apex of achievement to date, that only through
them—through their inspiration and effort—can
the Life Force achieve greater consciousness of
itself and reach that perfection which is eternally
its goal.

This is the basis of Shaw's creed, and the foundation of his philosophy. It is but the barest outline of
an outline of the new story of Creation, and only the
shadowy hint of a hint of the underlying process.
It is admittedly defective owing to the difficulty
of describing the activities of that which has no
attributes—a task to which it must be admitted
Shaw has unstintingly devoted himself. The story
has been found attractive. The cultured classes

39

had garbled versions of it in 1880, and nearly everyone has it to-day. There is in every day's news, in scientific journals, in all the best-sellers, and in the very latest religions, every evidence of its growing popularity.

This account of Creative Evolution at work through the Ages is, then, only a poor but honest attempt to make a preface to the Preface to *Back to Methuselah*, to which the reader is advised to go if he wishes to know what Shaw's creed is really like. Or he can go to Bergson and find :

" Life is the effort made by energy to become free. It uses the powers and properties of matter, storing itself up and releasing itself in free action and in so doing becoming ever more free. It first institutes movement in matter, and this movement having resolved itself into the solar system, among other things, life hits by a lucky chance on the chlorophyllian function as a means of storing up energy and releasing it in spurts and bursts of ' creativeness.' The impetus of life is finite, it has been given once for all, and must work its own way. It is a slow stumbling worker ever trying and failing and trying again."

Or to Rosenberg and read :

" A new sense of life which is conscious however of being rooted in the primitive past, pushes to the surface, and takes form ; a new view of life is born and begins to demand

40

> an account of ancient forms, sacred usages,
> and traditional values."

Or he may get the idea purged and refined in the
editorial pages of *Nature* (December 7th, 1935) :

> " Science has not only emancipated human
> thought from the bondage of traditional
> authority, but also, through the concept of
> evolution onward and upward, has provided
> mankind with a new philosophy of life."

If he is curious enough to go further, he will find
that Bergson, as becomes a philosopher, pursues his
way calmly, moulding his creation into shape with
pleasing, flowing words, but ever standing apart
from it ; while Rosenberg jumps into the arena and
spreads the Life Force story among a million readers
in the *Myth of the 20th Century*, impetuously telling
the tale of a new cell activity which is welding with
great blows of the Nordic hammer all plastic German
souls into one great race soul, and subordinating the
individual to the state ; to the dismay of *Nature's*
editor, who, in the upthrusting of the Life Force in
England, has just discerned the emancipation of
human thought from the shackles of authority.

But this search through the modes in which the
Life Force is expressing itself to-day leads only
through confusion into boredom, and it is better to
stick to Shaw, who never bores, however much he
may confuse. The other prophets are unbearably
dull as they go on and on ; he somehow manages to
say things which sound the same, but have a curious

41

freedom and elasticity of their own, as though he were standing despair on its head, and making it wave its legs in hope. He braces himself against the same base as the others, he shoots his arrows from the same citadel of modified Lamarck-Darwinism but he is different. He seems to have faith in what he is saying. The rest of them believe the Life Force story with about as much energy as they believe that the weather is going to be wet; they are careful not to allow belief to become mixed up with behaviour.

Shaw, on the other hand, seems at an early stage to have accepted this story of creation, or something like it, then to have said to himself : " Where do I come in ? " and to have seen that words alone could not answer that question. He gave his assent to the story, but instead of treating that as the end of the matter—going out and getting a good job as a journalist, and settling down to vegetate in comfort—he made his assent only the beginning, and with wild, indomitable logic, tried to conform his thoughts, words and actions to it. The " good job " was to him not living at all. Life was not a set of operations to be carried out according to rules laid down by London editors or even by the English upper classes. Life was he—Bernard Shaw—a man, alive, in a wonderful, ever-active world. But, so far as he could see, the sign-posts marked " This way to heaven " were all pointing in different directions. Way back about 1880 or earlier he

42

must have become aware of bewilderment and taken as a headline " Follow conscience for all you're worth." And then the fun began. It is an exciting headline for any man, but the tumult is usually a private matter ; in this case, with George Bernard Shaw hanging on to it for grim life, the results became a public spectacle for the world. No other prophet of Creative Evolution has risked the attempt to merge into one the cosmic story and the personal story. In his case the results have been given such labels as novels, pamphlets, plays, prefaces and letters, essays and tomfooleries, but such listing breaks up their unity and hides their meaning. From the early letters to *Public Opinion* in 1875, to the latest play in 1936, these writings are the scientific record of an extraordinary experiment in one-man living.

Sometimes the microscope is turned inwards, and sometimes outwards, but always the observations are made with the utmost care, and most faithfully recorded. This does not look like science because there is no laboratory, no mathematics, no chloro-formed kitten under a bell jar ; but any man who records his experiences accurately and honestly is a real scientist, and perhaps a poet as well. Shaw is a wonder as a first-hand observer and honest recorder, and his works are the results, disguised as plays and so on, covering an immense variety of experience. When he wants to say just what he feels and thinks about the particular specimen under observation, he writes a preface ; when he wants to hold up to the public a variety of other views plus his own, he writes a play. He ranges over everything freely, that is, freely within the limits of his creed. Other men write poems, plays and pamphlets in accordance with some prescribed formula, and get results fit for immediate embalming ; or else they write with absolute freedom, and get sentences which don't parse, written with words which aren't in the dictionary ; they try to get the Inner Light to do all the work, including the thinking. Shaw is prepared to say anything whatever, and to stand by the Inner Light through thick and thin, but he likes the practical record of his inspiration to stand to reason. His allegiance to reason is vigorously denied by large property owners, who can see nothing but madness in a well-to-do man saying that Russians are respectable, but he is really terribly reasonable in all secondary matters. There's only one author like him—a man who began with a page full of axioms and wrote books and books out of them—Euclid is inexorable. The man who accepts Euclid's axioms is done for, he must swallow every last bit of every single book to the last Q.E.D. His only chance is to say at the very beginning, " That last axiom looks crazy to me."

The point is that Shaw is true to his creed. It would have made things simpler for everyone if he had put his axioms on the first page like his great rationalist predecessor. That is why they are set out here at an early stage in the form of an account of creation, which can be examined at leisure. If Shaw is right about that he is right about everything else. Meanwhile, a lot of other questions arise. How did he come to believe such a story? Why did he throw overboard an extraordinary story about a whale, and then take up with a tall tale about a giraffe? What have evolutionary theories to do with play writing? What difference does a man's belief make to his day's work? Surely it's all a publicity ramp? What has conscience got to do with it? What's the use of bothering about beginnings? What does Shaw know about them? Who is Shaw?

CHAPTER III

HE is one of the Kilkenny–Dublin Shaws, friends of the great Ponsonbys. Sir John Ponsonby, a hard-headed firm-fisted north-of-England man, first came to Ireland with Cromwell as colonel in a cavalry regiment. He had all the qualities as soldier, business man, administrator and diplomatist neces-sary for acquiring lands during the Commonwealth, and holding them under the Restoration. The property passed to his son, Sir Henry, who, not being very sure of his ground under the Stuarts, backed William at the Battle of the Boyne, and established his position. His brother and heir, Sir William, finally consolidated the family fortunes, and ad-vanced into the Irish nobility, gaining the titles of Viscount Duncannon and Baron Bessborough.

This process of advancement was not accom-plished without loyal and willing help from Captain William Shaw of Hampshire, who came over and did his bit in Sir Henry's regiment at the Battle of the Boyne, and thereafter settled down in the shelter of the Bessborough estate on the southern border of County Kilkenny. The partnership, so happily begun in 1690, continued in the following genera-tions and the Shaws and Ponsonbys remained,

during the next century, in close and loyal
association in those pleasant lands north of the Suir,
where the salmon-fishing and fox-hunting were so
fine, and where the rich wines of the South could
be rolled cask by cask from the deck of the Portuguese
lugger up to the very door.

Those were wonderful days for the Shaws, in the
early eighteenth century, with the woods of Kilkenny
behind them, the sun slanting across the shadowy
Comeraghs down on the wide sweep of the river in
front, the rich land giving its store for all their needs
and a powerful patron over all. The savour of
them dwells in the pages of Somerville and Ross—
descendants of another of Cromwell's officers,
Colonel Bushe, who made his home in the next
pleasant valley a few miles away—as they write
of their great-grandfather, Charles Kendal Bushe :

"Kilkenny is a warm comfortable county,
of wide, rich pastures and wooded demesnes
and stately houses, with a big blue river running
swift and strong through its heart, the River
Nore, that has salmon to be caught that match
the river in speed and strength. Mountains it
has not, but there are hills that make a purple
margin for its landscapes, and above all the
other counties, it has trees, calm and superb,
with perfection undisturbed by such wind as
south-west Ireland knows. Kilfane and Kilmurray march together, and their boundary
line is buried in trees. Splendid oaks, serene

47

in unhindered growth ; chestnuts, that when I first saw Kilmurray were deep seas of green, with their myriad pale flowers like lamps reflected in troubled water : and beyond all other trees were the beeches, great domes of purple, some of them, but most were of the delicate shimmering green that is the lovely coming-out dress in which they meet the summer, and in their shade the wild bluebells were spreading like blue air between the grey trunks.

" Charles, who never missed a chance of getting on a horse, had gone for a morning ride. He had ridden into Kilmurray and galloped round the park. The lake that, so long ago, he had himself helped to plan and enlarge, was brimming. He jumped the little stream that fed it, and looked long at the reflection in the lake of the house he was born in " (*An Incorruptible Irishman*, p. 208).

It was splendid for the young men of those days to belong to such a county and to know that so many acres of it belonged to them ; but marriages were early, and there were children by the dozen, and in a few generations there was room only for the eldest, and younger sons began to be forced out, into military service and into the growing towns. Numbers of young Shaws had to leave the land, and branch out into respectable professions each generation. Two of these branches are full of interest.

The first springs from Robert Shaw, a fifth son, who left the old home in the 1760's, and became a very capable Accountant-General of the Post Office. His son Robert, born 1774, married an heiress in 1796 and by 1800 was showing his quality both in Parliament and in the comparatively new and interesting business of banking. He voted against the Union, when a vote on the other side was said to be worth anything from £30,000 to an earldom, and he steered his business through the financial straits of the early nineteenth century with such credit and profit that it became the basis of the Royal Bank of Ireland in 1836. He was made baronet in 1821. It is pleasant for those who see in the victory at the Boyne the beginnings of modern civilisation, to visualise young Captain William Shaw, on a white horse, charging the stricken enemy behind Sir Henry Ponsonby ; then to see them together later, so comfortably settled in their sylvan retreat ; then to see young Sir Robert standing, with four stalwart Ponsonbys, against the corruption of the Union ; and finally to find the old partnership commemorated generation after generation in Ponsonby Shaw (born 1784), sheriff and banker, Ponsonby Shaw (born 1810), lieutenant-colonel in the Madras army, and Ponsonby Shaw (born 1846) major in the late 95th Foot.

The other branch springs from Bernard Shaw, a third son, first cousin of the baronet, who left the old home in the 1790's, became a kind of lawyer-cum-broker, married a rector's daughter in 1802, and died in 1826, leaving behind an indomitable wife and fourteen children. How she managed to bring them up, as Henderson says : " in an unshaken and unshakable consciousness of their aristocracy," is one of the mysteries of those times, but it may be guessed that the banker-baronet, who provided a house for them in Terenure, was continuously helpful. Her third son, George Carr Shaw, married Lucinda Gurly in 1852, and settled down modestly at 3 Synge Street, Dublin.

At this house on July 26th, 1856, there was delivered that tender protoplasmic mass of curious, dim, Shaw-Gurly memories, enlivened by that entity incredibly new and free, which was to be called George Bernard and was to open self-conscious, observant eyes on the Dublin of the 'sixties.

A visitor to the Ireland of to-day will not find it difficult to reconstruct that Dublin. No. 3 Synge Street is now No. 33, and remains its box-like, yellow-bricked, basement-kitchened, granite-coped, bijou-Georgian self, the model of thousands built for genteel and not too well-to-do Dubliners, over a century ago. Behind the house the Grand Canal opened out into the Portobello Basin, from which the south city drew its drinking water, and on which the " Fly-boats " had rested a few years before, after their breathless dash up from Kildare at nine miles an hour, to discharge their passengers at the door of the Portobello Hotel. In 1850 William

Dargan was changing all that. He was building railways from the provinces to Dublin, and making a reputation for himself as a captain of industry, and the wealthiest man in Ireland. It was the age of Exhibitions ; eleven miles of stands of " all that was wonderful and exquisite " at the Crystal Palace were exciting the public mind, disturbing old conventions, stimulating new wants, rocketting industrialism, and making Ruskin and Morris wild. Fashionable Ireland wished to be in the swim, and Dargan, eager to help, was backing the first of the Dublin Exhibitons on Leinster Lawn in 1853. Dublin society was delighted, and supported it in the elegant, carefree, complimentary-ticket kind of way that has brought tears to the eyes of the guarantors of so many enterprises in that city, and in those days cost Dargan £26,000.

Within easy reach of Synge Street, in a house on Stephens Green, Cardinal Newman was planning a beautiful church and dreaming of a Catholic University while he looked out at the great open space, so suitable for his purpose, which lay between him and the newly built Harcourt Street Railway Station. But the idea of University materialises slowly, and while he thought and wrote, two young men named Guinness, to whom £26,000 was but petty cash, were looking at the site and making much faster progress with their idea of its suitability for exhibition purposes. It was taken over, a great hall was built, and in it were housed the Great

E 2

Dublin Exhibitions of 1865 and 1872. The stands were interesting.

The gas engine, telephone, and electric light were still unknown, but electro magnets had had their day, and city people were in a position to yawn politely when their country cousins chattered excitedly before models of the electric telegraph and the wonderful electric clock. Scientists had done wonders, but engineers and business men had not yet caught up, and so far there was little but rather clumsy dynamos to be seen. Still there was the wonderful sewing machine just beginning to come on the market in quantity, and a new material called rubber with amusing properties. A grey powder—Portland Cement—was being boosted as the building material of the future, to the unconcealed amusement of the brickmakers and quarry owners. There were great stands of Staffordshire pottery and rows and rows of chimney pieces in fine ironmongery and " a splendid array of gas fittings including gazaliers of various patterns, brackets and all the elegant modes of dispensing artificial light in society."

But nothing could surpass the thrill of the steam engine, with its whirling flywheel, and the maze of machines that could be made to dance attendance on it. It was old in the 'seventies, but still new. Even yet, there is something about that smooth flux of power under finger-tip control, which fascinates people as they watch the easy, powerful

52

pulse of the piston rod, and the curious baby-like sparring of the eccentrics. But in 1872 ! To think that never before in the history of the world had a locomotive been . . . and to be alive along with it ! To have been born into a horse-world, and to see the modern miracle of the railways spread out to take command of it ! Kipling was not yet under way, but the ideas he was to mould into poetry were already elusively dancing in the crowded aisles in those Exhibition years.

Young George Bernard Shaw seems to have been unmoved by the great shows going on so near him, as family ups and downs moved him first to a larger house, No. 1 Hatch Street, and then to lodgings in 61 Harcourt Street. At sixteen he was delving into books and music and more inclined to look ques-tioningly at the throngs passing down Earlsfort Terrace, then to go into raptures over " electro copies of great antique vases " or " work-boxes of mother of pearl." From his birth his home had been an unusual one, in which good music was as common as bread and butter, and used as freely and naturally. His mother had a lovely voice, and the aunt who had otherwise brought her up with such Puritan caution and rigour had recklessly given her an excellent musical education. She joined forces with a gifted music teacher, George Vandaleur Lee, and in No. 1 Hatch Street, Gounod, Verdi and Donizetti were as much at home as Tom, Dick and Harry in the ordinary household.

Shaw learnt music without consciousness of learning, as a child in a pleasant home learns good manners. His taste was nourished from the beginning, and the sensitiveness of his ear developed as naturally as the strength of his limbs. In due time came conscious knowledge, and the delight in widening it, ordering it, and making it at home which everyone who has ever gathered anything from stamps to stars can understand and share in a slight way. Clear understanding is not so easy, for there is something close and intimate here which rebels against analysis and is not easily amenable to reason ; see how music-minded people begin their discussions so courteously and end by just " going on " at one another. It will not do, then, to be too clever and psycho-analytical and lazy, and find the whole future springing from the over-development of one particular faculty, the encouragement of intense and unbalanced sensibilities, and the growth of a form of expression to give them an outlet when capacity for musical composition and performance was lacking. That would be pure speculative eyewash, and would rule out all the pleasant, human, interesting influences which contributed to the startling appearance, in London of the 'eighties, of a young man who not only knew what was wrong with the world, but also knew what to do about it. Still, the influence of music was fundamental ; the part it played is evident at every turn, in the trend of his thoughts, in his career and in his writings. The great composers were his earliest teachers, and their operas were his fairy tales, and from the beginning, there was a gulf between the boy to whom music was a native language to an inner ear, and the other boys to whom it was so much sound. It was a gulf which was to grow with every development of that sensitive discriminating ear, and to make him forever something of a stranger to the rest of us, to whom music is at best a pleasant noise which we can stand for a couple of hours at a time for culture's sake.

The story of those days will be found in the preface to his first novel, *Immaturity*. The preface was written forty years after the novel, and gains in pungency what it loses in the ill-balanced emphasis of a man of sixty-five writing of his youth. He seems to have mixed little with others of his age, and to have passed from childhood to manhood without that intermediate stage in which the male measures himself against other boys, and makes some essential adjustments during a period of physical destructiveness and general devilment. When other boys, in pairs and gangs, were breaking windows, laws and everything else that stood in their small ways, he was reading and following up with delight the antics of those wonderful figures which troop so readily into any young imagination which invites them. Reading and music went hand in hand to give material and impetus to the events of his dream worlds, and the great dramas going on around him seem to have been almost ignored. He was busy playing with the wonderful works men had created for his delight. It mattered not whether they were in words or music—the two flowed so easily in his mind that he scarce needed to distinguish them. Shelley must have come early. He had been in Dublin in the lifetime of Shaw's parents, enthroned in a balcony in O'Connell Street distributing pamphlets on world reform to the passers-by ; he was real, and his story was vivid, to cultured Dublin of the 'seventies ; and his message brimming in sense and sound, was an intoxicating draught for young George Bernard.

Poets and composers were his heroes, and his interest spread from them to the others, who created in colour and stone, and sent him in his teens wandering round the Dublin Art Galleries. It is small wonder he cared little for engines and mechanical things from factories, or for the mass activities of men. Only the individual—the craftsman—could produce this thing called beauty which stirred him so mysteriously and set him apart from the world which was making its first wild gropings towards mass production. He had no interest in the struggle between iron and steel, in which Henry Bessemer had just scored such a victory, nor could he get excited about the difference between basic and phosphoric ores, which was the essence of romance to the Gilchrists. He did not care in the least about the lack of standardisation in the

engineering industry ; he probably never even
heard of Whitworth nor of the efforts he was making
to get British manufacturers to realise the value of
exact measurement and precise standards. But
this is scarcely surprising ; neither he, nor anyone
but a few far-seeing business men, realised the close
connection between Whitworth's teaching and the
possibility of turning out guns and ammunition
more rapidly than men could fire them off. The
Crimean and American wars had just fizzled out
on old slow-going traditional lines, and Germany
was beginning to demonstrate the superiority of
the new mode in which rapid movement was
backed by equally rapid munition output, but to
Shaw-among-the-artists the Franco-Prussia war
was an event on the very margin of consciousness.

Neither he, nor his family, nor any of their class,
noticed the greater conflict going on nearer home.
It was a new form of the long-lasting Anglo-Irish
struggle in which the opposing forces were now
landlords and tenants. There had been a terrifying
engagement in the 'forties, in which the mortality
of the tenants and their families reached 900,000.
The landlords called this " The Great Famine "
and continued to press for rent, complaining of the
disaffection and ingratitude of the lower classes,
and calling occasional casualties which occurred
among themselves " dastardly murders." *The
Times* of 1872 speaks for them :

> The Imperial legislature should endeavour
> to govern each individual section of the immense
> population under its sway, as those composing
> it would wish to govern themselves, supposing
> them to be sufficiently enlightened to wish
> well. . . . Ireland is now governed as nearly
> as possible . . . as we might suppose Ireland
> to govern herself were she in her right mind.

This did not raise even a smile in the Shaw household. George Carr Shaw had an acute and mischievous sense of humour, but anything touching
the prestige of the class to which he belonged, was
sacred. He looked on the wretched Irish as a
separate species, and did his utmost to save his son
from contact with them. The very existence of
the Ponsonby-Shaw class hung on this conviction of
their superiority to the mere Irish ; it was often
combined with kindness and consideration of the
quality sometimes shown to domestic animals :
see, in the novels of Lover and Lever, how benignly
the culture and elegance of the quality contrasts
with the crudity and credulity of the native ; their
faith in the eternal propriety of this contrast was
about all that remained of the Puritan doctrines
of former days, and their religion consisted mainly
of some good social habits turning about a belief
that the elect were always well-dressed and lived
in well-kept houses. They lived on the assurance
that a rather irritable God, who was displeased
with the Irish for their loyalty to his predecessor,

had presented their forefathers with the Bible as a legal instrument entitling them to hold all the best land and best jobs in the country. They brought up their families carefully under a code consisting of some of the solid old virtues merged in a wonderful mixture of pious practices, family customs, prejudices and conventions, all firmly bonded into a sense of their own impeccability and superiority. They had a general feeling that the existence of their God could be proved from the Bible, and they accepted the Ussher chronology and Milton's lion with his hairy mane and clay tail, as absolute and final truth ; they were very close to their ancestors of the seventeenth century.

Shaw's parents had been moulded in their youth by some such upbringing and teaching into the standard pattern, but ideas abroad in the 'sixties and unfortunate events in their own lives, upset them. His father was a kindly, weakly man, who had been given a start in life by influential friends, but he was incapable of settling down seriously to hard work in the flour-milling business. He was probably obsessed with the notion that a Kilkenny Shaw should not have to work—even in Wholesale. All his life he was dogged by complexes. He wanted to drink, but believed that drinking was sinful and ruined so many promising parties by beginning to lament his miserable condition just when everyone else was getting into good form, that he was finally dropped socially. The man was overwhelmed by the Puritan on the drink question, but he would not take a beating ; he popped up in another field and revenged himself. When the Puritan threatened George Carr with specially picked texts about the elect and the damned, he pointed to *The Origin of Species* in 1859, and *The Antiquity of Man* in 1863, and put his fingers to his nose. Still, he was never very sure of himself, and compromised by earnestly teaching his son to respect the Bible and at the same time encouraging his ribald young efforts at higher criticism with uproarious laughter.

Mrs. Shaw was made of sterner stuff. Her son says : " Her character reacted so strongly against her strict and loveless training, that churchgoing was completely dropped in our family before I was ten years old " (*Prefaces*, p. 633). She never seems to have taken any further interest in the severe teachings of her Calvinistic aunt, or to have been impelled to teach her son anything but love for the music in which she immersed herself when she became disappointed with her husband's feebleness, and disgusted with his morose conviviality. It is probable that George Carr's high and mighty attitude about the Shaws and their great connections bred in her a satirical outlook on men and their ways, which she unconsciously passed on to her son. She was a woman of strong personality and decisive character, and she must have exercised a multitude of influences of this kind, but she seems to have

felt little responsibility towards him, and generally
to have left him to his own resources.

There was no one at No. 1 Hatch Street to treat
him as a boy looking out on a new and surprising
world, or as a small person with some right to an
intelligible explanation of why he had been invited
into it. It was a house of grown-ups, who passed
on their adult viewpoints to him, as if he were a
little replica of themselves, and he was left to
struggle as best he could to make sense of his father's
divided counsels, his mother's cool detachment,
his uncle William's waverings between piety and
bathing beauties, his uncle Walter's brilliant blas-
phemies, and the way in which a group of be-
whiskered men could argue for hours on the possibility of miracles, after starting with the assumption that they couldn't happen. They made no
allowance for the fierce logic of childhood which
was for some reason working in a more uncom-
promising way than usual in their midst, as young
George Bernard strove to arrange the sensations
which were pouring in upon him, so that the real
world would be orderly and beautiful like the
dream worlds of his imagination. He was at last
taking an interest in something outside himself.
This Religion *versus* Science controversy which was
spreading like wildfire in England and reflected in
so many discussions in his home, made instant appeal
to him. It was a dispute full of mighty drama and
human interest, alive with the vigour of the great

personalities involved, and as he listened to the
faint echoes of it which reached Dublin, and eagerly
read the latest proofs that the world was more than
6,000 years old, he easily made his decision. He
would be a champion of this fresh, vivid, certain
knowledge against the shams and crudities of religion. He had no experience of science, and the
only religion of which he had inside knowledge
was the one his family had turned down before he
was ten, but he was full of that glorious assurance
which has never left him. He saw clearly facts and
common sense on one side, and delusion and
hypocrisy on the other, and made his choice,
scarcely knowing at first that it was a choice.

This matter of choice was strange. He had known
about it vaguely for years, but about this time—
say 1870—his knowledge opened out into wonderful
discovery. He found out that he was alone in a
new and exciting way—as though George Bernard
was floating off on his own, and had his eye on
young Shaw. He found that he was something
apart from his mother, father, uncles, aunts, and
the Shaw tradition ; that he need not think as
they thought, nor do as they did, nor even do as he
did yesterday. He was not only new—he was free,
and not only free to think, but to make a choice
this way or that and to act. Just here there was a
strangeness, for the wonderful intangible freedom
had a direction and in some indescribable way it
was found possible to act for, and to act against.

62

He was free and not free at the same time. He was in some way responsible, in some way required to act reasonably. He was not allowed to have all the fun of thinking and coming to conclusions without acting on them. He could, of course, turn them down if he liked, but it would make him uncomfortable; on the other hand, if he brought his conclusions out into the open by action, there was this indescribable feeling of lightness, freedom, and power. George Bernard had discovered his conscience.

Conscience was at a discount in those days. In Germany it had just been analysed as a compound of fear, superstition, prejudice, vanity, and custom. In England it was argued that it was only a spasm of the diaphragm like a sneeze or a cough, or else held to be a by-product of the social process still of value among primitive peoples, but no longer so necessary at home, owing to the British Constitution, the Bank of England, and the Police. In Dalkey, Ireland, a boy was ignoring all this modern teaching, and beginning to experiment on himself; he had discovered his conscience, and was getting ready to back it against the world.

Every year the Shaws sought relief from the heat, the dust, and the flat, flat flatness of South Dublin City, in a summer holiday at Dalkey. Synge Street and Hatch Street lie low within the curve of the canal, encased in dull brick fronts and dreadful iron-railed basements. The district is still a favourite gathering place for the mild mists of the city, and by some trick of the atmosphere or the landscape, the horizon on dull days seems to lie at arm's length. Heaven and earth are flattened out. The very sky seems to rise out of the ground, and to press down on tree-tops and roofs like a great grey cover. By the canal, the stimulus of Mozart and the colour and movement of the Arabian Nights could only be matched by scenery of the imagination. At Dalkey it was different. To know the difference you must make a pilgrimage to Synge Street, walk along Heytesbury Street to Bride Street, look at Molyneux Church where Shaw received weekly instruction for a time, and then cut across through the slums to Stephens Green and Leeson Street. After that tour of a two-dimensional world, take a swift run to Dalkey—only eight miles away—and climb Torca Hill.

Torca Cottage, where the Shaws used to stay, is still there, but new buildings and new walls make it more difficult now to wander at will about the summit. For the rest, there is no change since Druid and Danish days in the wonders of land, sea, and sky, that lie so lavishly around. From morning till night in those long summer days, a boy was able at last to open his eyes and see something that was in keeping with that incessant imperious demand for beauty and more beauty ; for beauty that would sweep and surge on, and yet be unchanged ; that would match his leaping imagination and yet stun it into breathless helplessness. . . .

The mail-boat harbour lies like a child's toy below. On the west of the hill are the two great quarries which built it. There is a spot above the rocky precipice at the end of one of them—a nice dangerous ledge that a boy would love. The wind comes brushing along the green quarry floor, meets the granite face, and pours wildly, escapingly, over that ledge, full of deep, soft, untiring music and a song of one word. The briar, the whitethorn, and the gorse that have somehow managed to find a home in the granite, dance wildly in the whirling eddies, and the hawkbit tosses hundreds of golden heads about, deliriously and yet deliciously in time with the slow beat of that throbbing word. Sweeping round the shoulder of Kilmashogue comes the wind, with all the richness gathered in the heather lands and cornfields of Kildare, to toss it up to the sky over Torca Head, and pour it down in wild abandonment over Killiney Bay. It is the busiest wind in the world, searching, sweeping, grooming, tidying every inch of that cliff face. Under the great booming organ note, there is the tenderest bustling hissing as it works on tendrils, twigs and leaves ; colour, sound and movement are one ; softness, wantonness, warmth, blend into speed and energy that mocks the anchored granite. Heady stuff for a boy fresh from Shelley and brick-bounded streets !

Fifty yards away on the south slope he could sit on the soft turf in the shelter of a great sparkling boulder and watch the sea spreading in grey-green lights and shadows to its twenty-mile horizon. The wind's music softens to the very borders of silence, and a murmur of surf breaking comes up from the white lacy frill that wavers along the miles of pebbly beach to Bray. Everything down there moves with a curious slow deliberation, as if by careful arrangement. The seagulls hang like the lightest of floating feathers, and the waves move on slowly to their appointed places, the lazy whiteness creeps monotonously up and down Killiney Strand, holding the eye, numbing the mind, and gripping the heart with despairing delight. That soft unceasing caress of land and waters is alive with some secret, telling it openly again and again, and yet hiding it maddeningly behind the changes which leave it ever new and unchanged.

But the wind and the sea and the lovely sweep up from the strand across the vale of Shanganagh to the mountains beyond are all suddenly forgotten playthings. Reaching down to those mountain tops is a sky which is like no other sky. It rises in great billowing grey rain-clouds over War Hill and races round the Bay in enormous curving shadows to change its mood to mighty piled-up snowy masses beyond Howth, and die away at last in soft pale lavender tones over Balbriggan. It is not one, but many skies, stormy and calm, cloudy and clear, endlessly blending into one another. The hill-top is in the midst of an airy

sea alive with stirring light, and full of bewildering
variety, against that serenity of eternal blue. In
the evening all that contrasting beauty intensifies
and focuses about the dull furnace glow over the
western plain ; behind Howth the towering masses
of the day have disappeared, and a motherly sky
is putting a sleepy land to bed with fold on fold of
cloud, so lazily, so expertly, spread out. Above, a
few scattered patches of silver-grey are tiredly
trying a few last cloud measures in the dimmer and
dimmer light.

Down below, wandering among the gorse, young
Bernard in his teens was embarking on his great
venture on some such night as this. It might have
happened anywhere, and it is possible that those
pure, soaring, spacious skies had nothing whatever
to do with it, but suddenly he was taking stock of
himself, and finding, to his discomfort, that he was
thoroughly two-faced. It was out on Torca Hill
in the dusk of a summer's evening, when colour had
gone from the sky, and a few slight stars were out,
that young George Bernard suddenly found himself
taking stock of Shaw, and urging him to mend his
ways. He had become conscious, at last, that old
habits did not tally with new thoughts, and he
suddenly decided he wasn't going to have it.
Something was forcing him to be honest and he was
facing the issue with a primitive simplicity unknown
to the Shaws, who always asked : " What would
the Ponsonbys think ? " He was taking up his

stand on completely new ground with the query :
" What's the good thing to do ? " The Science-
Religion controversy which was going on about
him with such intensity had suddenly become a
personal issue ; he was aware at last that he had
made a choice, and he was bringing his conscience
to bear on it as easily and naturally as a bird flies
when it is time for it to fly. He was saying in so
many words : " Truth is good—religion is a sham—
therefore religious practices are evil," and there
and then he decided he must give up his prayers.
It was a bit of a wrench, for he was fond of his night
prayers, and made a feature of them in his own
picturesque way, but he could not go on with them.
They were magic, mockery, a bad habit, and he
must give them up. Many a boy would have
compromised and slowed off by degrees, but there
was something unrelentingly scrupulous about this
lad which made thought and action one, and there
and then he turned his back on the God of his
fathers. Lest there be any mistake in this description of a crucial decision and the manner of it, here
is his own story :

> I continued these pious habits long after
> the conventional compulsion to attend church
> and Sunday School had ceased, and I no longer
> regarded such customs as having anything to
> do with an emancipated spirit like mine. But
> one evening as I was wandering in the furze
> bushes on Torca Hill in the dusk, I suddenly

asked myself why I went on repeating my prayer every night, when, as I put it, I did not believe in it. Being thus brought to book by my intellectual conscience, I felt obliged in common honesty to refrain from superstitious practices ; and that night for the first time since I could speak, I did not say my prayers (*Prefaces*, p. 633).

There never was a more logical man. He began with that fateful syllogism on Torca Hill, and from that day to this he has never ceased trying to fit himself into it ; even when he dropped materialism, which he did years afterwards, as promptly and scrupulously as he dropped his prayers, he tried to make a religion which would square with it—a religion without rules or practices.

It is hard for the average decent Englishman to realise the artificiality of the conventions which held together the one-sided civilisation of Protestant Ireland in the 'seventies, and the stunning effect of the new truths which Haeckel, Spencer, Huxley and Tyndall were preaching with such intensity and ability. But it is easy for everyone to delight in the fresh impetuous vigour with which young George Bernard began to use his natural gifts, trying to bring some order into the queer world into which he had been landed. He was proud of his new knowledge of himself, and delighted in the freedom and sense of power which it gave. This wonderful self-consciousness and exercise of his rational appetite opened a new world, and he found himself looking curiously at others in the light of it, and embarking on discussions to find out what their worlds were like. The orthodoxy of his acquaintances rested on peculiar foundations, and as he probed, in arguments at the office and elsewhere, loss of temper on their part and increasing conviction on his, easily followed. He became more and more cool and certain, as they became hotter and more abusive, and he began to observe human behaviour with an increasingly critical eye. Out of his discovery of himself there slowly grew the further discovery that most men lived on their habits and prejudices, and didn't like being asked " Why ? " From his point of view they were hardly alive at all, for " Why " and " Why not " were the very food of his life. He began to suspect all conventions, and found himself looking at people and events as though he had come from another planet and was seeing them for the first time.

He had a clerical position in an estate office in Molesworth Street, where he carried out his duties punctiliously, instructed his fellow clerks in musical matters, and got a reputation as an atheist. In the early seventies he was living at 61 Harcourt Street, where his father had moved when the family broke up and his mother went to London. Outside the office he gave much time to music and science ; music he studied by listening and playing, but his knowledge of science was unfortunately gained from books. He had no notion of what he was letting himself in for, nor of his complete helplessness in the hands of any scientific writer with a good style and a pet theory ; there were some wonderful expositors in those days, and Tyndall, who was at the British Association meeting in Belfast in 1874, was one of the best ; his presidential address was disturbing to many, but thrilling to his young admirer in Dublin. It went like this : " The mild light of Science breaking in upon the minds of the youth of Ireland is a surer check to any spiritual tyranny which might threaten this island than the laws of princes and the swords of emperors," and like this : " In matter we discern the promise and the potentiality of all terrestial life. The doctrine of evolution derives man in his totality from the interaction of organism and environment through countless ages past." It is hard to believe now that this balanced phrasing was spell-binding in 1874, and that its confident tone carried conviction to millions. But in those days atoms were ultimates. It was useless to try to peer beyond them, for they were hard and unchanging—like billiard balls—banking up the farthest frontiers of knowledge with an impenetrable wall ; and anyhow, peering was unnecessary, for, with a limited selection of atoms, a few simple laws and an æon or two, it was possible to show that everything came about quite naturally. In controversy with an obstinate opponent the atoms could always be backed up by "immutable, inexorable laws," with good effect. Billiards was said to be a sinful game, and it was pleasant for boys to be able to get a reputation for wickedness and at the same time have a secret conviction that they were being virtuous, and learning about the Unknowable every time they brought off a clever cannon. Young Bernard was far too serious-minded and hard-up a boy to waste his time at billiards, but he was giving much thought to cause and effect, hard facts, and the problem of finding rational explanations for all human behaviour; his satirical feeling against the respectable classes was growing and he was spoiling for a chance to show what was in him. He got it when Moody and Sankey visited Dublin, and he felt called to give some rational comment on revivalism. His letter on this matter has fortunately been rescued by Mr. Henderson from the copy of *Public Opinion*, dated April 3rd, 1875.

"Sir,

"In reply to your correspondent 'J. R. D.,' as to the effect of the ' wave of evangelism,' I beg to offer the following observations on the late ' revival ' in Dublin, of which I was a witness.

"As the enormous audiences drawn to the evangelistic services have been referred to as a proof of their efficacy, I will enumerate some of the motives which induced many persons to go. It will be seen that they were not of a religious, but a secular, not to say profane, character.

" Predominant was the curiosity excited by the great reputation of the evangelists, and the stories widely circulated, of the summary annihilation by epilepsy and otherwise of sceptics who had openly proclaimed their doubts of Mr. Moody's divine mission.

" Another motive exhibits a peculiar side of human nature. The services took place in the Exhibition Building, the entry to which was connected in the public mind with the expenditure of a certain sum of money. But Messrs. Moody and Sankey opened the building ' for nothing,' and the novelty, combined with the curiosity, made the attraction irresistible.

" I mention these influences particularly as I believe they have hitherto been almost ignored. The audiences were, as a rule, respectable ; and as Mr. Moody's orations were characterised by an excess of vehement assertion and a total absence of logic, respectable audiences were precisely those which were least likely to derive any benefit from them.

" It is to the rough, to the outcast of the streets, that such ' awakenings ' should be addressed, and those members of the aristocracy who by their presence tend to raise the meetings above the sphere of such outcasts are merely diverting the evangelistic vein into channels where it is wasted, its place being already supplied, and as, in the dull routine of hard work, novelty has a special attraction for the poor, I think it would be well for clergymen, who are nothing if not conspicuous, to render themselves so, in this instance, by their absence.

" The unreasoning mind of the people is too apt to connect a white tie with a dreary church service, capped by a sermon of platitudes, and is more likely to appreciate ' the gift of the gab '—the possession of which by Mr. Moody nobody will deny—than that of the Apostolic Succession, which he lacks.

" Respecting the effect of the revival on individuals I may mention that it has a tendency to make them highly objectionable members of society, and induces their unconverted friends to desire a speedy reaction, which either soon takes place or the revived one relapses slowly into his previous benighted condition as the effect fades, and although many young men have been snatched from careers of dissipation by Mr. Moody's exhortations, it remains doubtful whether the change is not merely in the nature of the excitement rather than in the moral nature of the individual. Hoping that these remarks may elucidate further opinions on the subject.

" I remain, Sir, yours, etc.,

" S."

His age was just eighteen years and eight months.

74

CHAPTER IV

THE writer of that letter was clearly not the stuff that elderly estate clerks are made from, and it is not surprising to find him dropping his job in the following year and going to live with his mother and sister in London. He was ill at ease in Dublin in more ways than one. He had probably missed his mother's company, her music and her clear-headed common sense more than he realised ; he didn't like office work, and he wanted to escape before it closed about him permanently as a means of livelihood ; he was a very conscientious young Atheist trying to reconcile a sincere belief that he was entirely due to molecules and immutable law, with a keen sense of humour, and it was difficult for him to find congenial company. He probably didn't know quite what he wanted. The story that he went to London to become a writer, because London is the hub of the world in which the English language is used, seems thin, and it is likely that he was as mixed in his motives for actions as a young man of twenty generally is, and made the break mainly because he wanted something to happen, and knew that it wouldn't, so long as he remained in Dublin.

He had entered the land office at the age of fifteen as an office boy, and carried out duties of increasing responsibility for four and a half years, to the complete satisfaction of his employer. He was in a position to learn much about land, money and credit, but the transactions of commerce didn't interest him any more than the swiftly-changing political drama going on about him. An acre of land and its meaning in terms of potatoes or fodder had no significance for him, rent was just something difficult to collect, and money just a row of figures in a ledger. His work was so much grind painstakingly done, and outside of it there was art—music, pictures, books—to stir and delight his ardent young mind, and give him more and more food for speculation about men and women, and their gifts, activities and relationships to one another. He was an efficient clerk with no more interest in the machine he was helping to operate than the average motorist has in cam design. He didn't even know it was a machine, though he was unconsciously gaining exact experience of it, and storing up at first hand the knowledge which was to be unleashed with such stark effect in *Widowers' Houses*. He didn't know that he was a child trying to live in a world of commerce and investment which had no use for new life.

London in 1876 was the very centre of that world. Enterprises of every kind converged there in search of credit, and spread out in practical form over the seas of the world. Iron ships, barely known in 1850, were steaming everywhere, speeding up interchanges, cutting costs and multiplying profits. England was building them, manning them, coaling them, and filling them with the cargoes of manufactured goods for which those countries which had managed to line their pockets with London loans, were crying out. Investments abroad rose from £230,000,000 in 1850 to £1,200,000,000 in 1875. To the Forsytes of those days it seemed that all the ages of the world were but a preparation for this great age of Victoria, and that at last in their lifetime, mankind, with England well in the van, had arrived at a suitable resting-place, fair and level, after the painful upward struggle of centuries. Some of the highbrow Forsytes could even look back in the light of the new knowledge, over dim stretches of millions of years, and breathe grateful acknowledgments to the amœba, the first fish, and the last superlative monkey for their various contributions to this wonderful condition of assured prosperity and established security. They easily passed to the stage of looking on their possessions and institutions as the final fruit of the evolutionary effort of the ages, and strove with every domestic and political nerve to establish themselves permanently in their thickly draped, heavily furnished, tremendously solid homes. Young Soames Forsyte was taught the doctrine of property by the very canopy on his cradle, and the way his uncles spoke to their wives.

77

The Prime Minister, Disraeli, who understood London business men even better than he understood the Queen, was giving them every help that could be expected from a practical politician. His shrewdness about the Suez Canal had brought him great prestige. Bankers, shipping companies, eastern traders, and the great investing public loved him, and the London Press was solidly behind him. But he had to be friendly with Turkey, and the position became very involved when Achmet Aga was decorated by the Sultan for burning twelve hundred Christians alive in a church. Gladstone "came back" with a pamphlet, *Bulgarian Horrors and the Question of the East*, which was bought up at once through the country, but coldly received in the House of Commons, where all those with even a remote financial interest in the East thought the time for action inopportune. Domestic affairs in the Balkans were the topic of the day, and subjects like housing conditions in Lancashire were never even mentioned ; everyone knew the meaning of *bashi-bazouk*, but the meaning of back-to-back houses was only known to landlords and building contractors. Atrocities abroad were more exciting than rickets at home, and Turkey held the centre of the stage till suddenly, in 1878, the Glasgow Bank failed for £6,000,000 and bankruptcy and unemployment spread over the whole country in the great slump of 1879. The eyes of England came back from the ends of the earth ; the Forsytes and their factory managers, hard driven by even harder driven bank managers, said : " Business as usual," and made ends meet by discharging surplus employees, cutting wages and extending hours, and the " lower classes " saved the country's credit by tightening their belts and living on the edge of starvation for a year. But their marvellous good nature was badly strained, and some patient murmurs were rising ; they were rather confused and illiterate murmurs, for the population had risen from sixteen to twenty-four millions in twenty-five years, and there was no money left for schools and teachers when £970,000,000 had been spent abroad. The murmurs from below might have died away, or been choked out, had they not been joined by some terrific roars from above, from men neither patient nor illiterate ; Ruskin's outpourings were beginning to tell, Morris was getting so wild at the growing ugliness about him that he could think of nothing but blowing it all up in one glorious explosion, Marx had written a book half full of terrible indisputable facts about industrialism, which a few men were beginning to read. But the polite world paid little attention to these people.

In 1880 Gladstone was back in the saddle. He wanted to do something to help the " lower classes " ; they were so patient and good-natured, and it was a shame to see so many of them starving and diseased. But he didn't get a chance to attend to England. In Ireland the polite world had been

trying to keep the fashionable pace set in London
without having any foreign orders for cotton goods,
coal or locomotives to help them, and the "lower
classes" had lost their good nature and were
beginning to shoot; worse still, Irish members
were beginning to be guilty of grave indecorum in
the House of Commons. Parnell was coming into
power. He had entered the House in 1875 in the
same cool, appraising way that Shaw entered
London a year later; he had seen Joe Biggar
obstructing public business in a villainous way;
he had heard him say, "Butt's a fool. He's too
gentlemanly. We are all too gentlemanly," and he
had immediately agreed with Biggar. Public
opinion was shocked—a quiver of horror ran round
the Stock Exchange—London editors exchanged
significant looks—a young man had come into the
English House of Parliament for the first time, and
was not impressed.

In five years Butt had gone under, saying, "I am
not in favour of a policy of exasperation," and
Parnell, rising to leadership on the wings of that
policy, was making the Irish question hum. Since
1850 tenants had been making mild protests against
starvation. Their leaders had begun by saying
"Property has its duties as well as its rights," and
been rebuked by an English peer for preaching
Communism. They continued to go on in this
cautious, good-humoured way till, in 1878, Michael
Davitt, a man from Mayo who had been given

years for reflection in Dartmoor Gaol, came out with a slogan that settled the whole question. Once he stood up at Irishtown in 1879 and said, "The land for the people," the game was up. Everyone knows what happened next, and it is all another story.

The important point here is that while the stage was being set during the period 1876–1880 for the Imperialist, Labour, Irish and Socialist struggles which followed, young Shaw, at the very centre of affairs, took no real interest in it. The political situations at home and abroad were full of dramatic tension, and were a common topic in all circles, the newspapers of the time were full of them; yet —in these four years, between the ages of twenty and twenty-four—he ignored public affairs. It wasn't that he didn't notice them: he noticed everything. Nor that he was preoccupied with efforts to earn his living: the only thing he feared was that some influential friend might lure him into a job. Nor that he was busy looking after his mother and sister: emotional domesticities were unknown in the Shaw home. Nor that he was seeing life with some of the lads: he had no money, and, anyhow, could he have stood their company and they his? No, he took no interest in the worlds of business or politics, not because of minor distractions, but because he was preoccupied with something vastly more impressive and exciting than the magnificence of Gladstone or the manœuvres of

Bismarck. He was wondering what he would do about George Bernard Shaw.

The fellow was a tremendous responsibility. Every baby knows that he is important. He is born with that conviction and carries it with him till such time as it is harnessed, or enslaved, or deformed by matter-of-fact elders with an eye to the main chance, or by murderous mass output educational systems designed to mould him to a particular pattern and produce a social unit which will not ask questions or "cause trouble." George Bernard had not been properly moulded, and that primary intuition had not been blotted out or obscured by some small-scale political or financial ambition. It roamed all over the place, and though occasionally toying with the notion of outclassing Michael Angelo, it preferred not to be tied down by any limitations. He was, in fact, George Bernard and Company, Unlimited, and the Company was stupendous. Bunyan was jostling Michael Angelo, Huxley and Helmholtz were crowding on top of Shakespeare and Beethoven, Dickens and Wagner were trying to make themselves at home, Shelley had come to stay. At first it was enough to be entertained and to soar off on the wings of each of them in turn; he and the artist and the delights unfolded were one. But later these men and the wonders they made became elusive, at one moment he possessed them, and they him, and the next they were apart and remote, outside of him and inaccessible. More puzzling still, he himself split up, he could read and roam with Al Raschid and at the same time look back curiously from Baghdad at the boy in Hatch Street turning over the pages with such eager intensity ; he used to wonder which was which. He had found that he could get outside and look at himself ; he could think about his thoughts. He suddenly knew piercingly that he was himself, that in all time there had never been anything like him. He knew he was new ; the intuition had come out into the open, he had been right all along, he was indeed something marvellous . . . like every other boy. They all know it at times, but he knew it more steadily and keenly than most, and he would not let that glorious vision fade ; with him it became every day fresher and more enthralling.

He was wildly curious and gradually began to turn himself into that miraculous microscope in which he was at once the observer, the instrument, and the specimen. Usually George sat stiff, serious, intense at the eyepiece, and Bernard lay on the slide kicking up his heels ; he was always amused at George's attempts to get clear definition and finality. George was the organiser and looked down soberly, saying : " If you don't mind your step, you can't see where you are going," and the other tumbled about on his back chuckling : "If you don't look up you can't see at all."

He knew he was important with a simplicity of knowing which defies all trite and laborious analysis.

The conviction was not wrapped up in any particular aim or accomplishment like climbing Everest or sinking all ten-foot putts. It would have been just as intense had he been alone in his shirt on a raft in mid-ocean. It was no matter of assessment, depending upon some particular power; it didn't mean that he was more important than anyone else, it had nothing to do with outside things or people, it was sheer primal certainty. He was as sure of it as he was puzzled by it, and as determined to express it openly in some way as he was conscious of his absurd limitations. Linked with his conviction, almost identical with it, there was that intense sensitive scrupulousness. He would not do routine clerical work because it was a waste of himself, yet when he was trapped into a job he performed his duties most punctiliously lest he take wages which were not fully due to him. He must preserve his identity, his sense of himself, his freedom, at all costs, and to this end he scrutinised all his actions, pouncing unmercifully on all unworthy motives, and trying with all the earnestness of his twenty-one pure and fervent years to be a perfectly rational being.

He was for ever trying to see what it was all about, and particularly what he was for. It had seemed clearer in Dublin as he graduated amid the concerts, the bookstalls, the picture galleries and the skies of Torca Hill. Now, taking his post-graduate course in the reading-room of the British Museum, in the London parks and galleries, and in various musical

84

drawing-rooms, he became less assured, but no less determined to use himself mightily in some way. That was what all those great ones had done, and he wanted to be like them, or rather—for imitation was anathema—to do something which would make him of their company. He didn't want to be like anyone but George Bernard Shaw, who was now, after a year or two in London, getting restless because nothing was being done about him. He was chock-full of booklearning, miscellaneous sensations, and wild fancies; of theories about music, painting, and literature; and he was simmering with the excitements of his microscopic research on himself and others. There was nothing for it but to write a book. At worst it would give George and Bernard some regular occupation and an outlet, and keep them from wrecking their prim Shaw-Gurly home.

The book was finished in 1879. It is a remarkable work of 140,000 words, every one of them selected with the greatest care and neatly fitted in place; on every page is stamped this impression of sentences deliberately chosen word by word to etch a special shade of meaning, and marshalled as carefully as the figures in a ledger. After an opening reminiscent of Dickens, he settles down to work in a way completely his own; he writes to no model, he has, in his sweet innocence or insolent independence, no publisher or public in view; he is not writing a novel for sale; he is making a work of art. It is an amazing book. It is like a picture in which the

artist worked from top to bottom, putting in every
object he had ever seen with faithful skill; or like
the first lesson given by a new teacher who covers
the session's syllabus in a single hour. It is full of
himself at his most threefold, eagerly filling the
stage, cautiously prompting from the wings and
critically scoffing from the stalls. He ranges everywhere, producing a curious impression of time
running backwards in a sort of inverted condensed
recapitulation, with the theme of *Major Barbara*
dimly appearing and Jack Tanner struggling for
utterance. It is quite unreadable in the ordinary
way, for nothing happens, and the characters slip
in and out of focus all the time; but it is full of
interest, for it tells what George Bernard Shaw was
thinking about in 1878.

He brings characters on and off, for the sole
purpose of reviewing his interests, discussing his
problems and lecturing on his conclusions; they
deliver themselves in mighty conversational mouth-
fuls two pages at a time (he must have loved pouring
out his opinions like this from the day he learnt to
handle a pen). He covers every ordinary human
interest—sex, art, and religion predominating;
science is treated with what might almost be
described as deference, and it would appear that the
doctrine of the man from the molecule has been
accepted as basic truth beyond discussion. He
launches out early with an attack on evangelicalism:
" there arose a young man, earnest and proud of his

oratory, who offered up a long prayer in the course of which he suggested such modifications in the laws of nature as would bring the arrangement of the universe into conformity with his own tenets," and thereafter sallies on similar lines dot the pages. Towards the end there is a study of a neurotic convert to Catholicism ; the attack on revealed religion is naïvely made against a weak and tottering opposition and it is clear that he is trying to deal fairly with some typical supporters of a fast vanishing superstition. His manner with the types he introduces is olympian, he presents them with the urbane detachment and serene amusement of a Chinese philosopher ; there is not a trace of arrogance, not a single spiteful reference, as he sets his pious people on their feet and puts them through their pre-determined paces ; he respects the individuality of his cardboard creations ever at their feeblest.

There are solid slabs of discussion on literature, painting and music, which have nothing to do with the story and throw it out of balance with weight of unexpected expert knowledge. Music is always touched with a sure hand, and there is a studiously speculative interest in painting with some leaning towards Italian Primitives. For the rest, it is evident that the bookshelves of the British Museum were being ransacked daily for light on the heretics, critics, and querists of the past. Some of the discussions between the principals, Robert Smith and Harriet Russell, are less concerned with their affairs than with the author's latest dip into Rousseau or La Rochefoucauld.

Robert and Harriet are real people in a peculiar way. They move through imaginary scenes and situations with the stiffness of mechanical toys, but every now and then there is a spurt of vitality. Robert stands out clearly and contradictorily, at once puzzled and confident, lost in self-consciousness and acutely observant. It is the picture of a very young genius painted by himself, which will live as long as *Man and Superman*. Harriet is a mystery woman ; Robert is restless, but she barely moves ; every time she speaks, someone is flattened out. As the Scotch dressmaker of the story, she is hopeless, but as a series of oracular protests against males and their ways, she is very much alive. Listen to her sizing up Robert : " You are clever enough to argue for all you do, and I fear that is all the good your cleverness will ever be to you." It sounds very much like Mrs. Shaw's voice here and again in the wonderful summing up at the end : " You are not a boy ; and you are not grown-up. Some day you will get away from your books and come to know the world and get properly set. But just now there is no doing anything with you. You are just a bad case of immaturity." Robert replies from his heart : " I never could feel grown-up ; and I believe you were born grown-up. I am afraid I am incurable."

The trouble about Robert was that no one ever called him Bob, he was at once too young and too old, and he *would* ask such queer questions ; even when he was courting, his curiosity got the better of him. " Are you fond of dressmaking ? " asked Smith, wishing to discover how far she had the feeling of an artist about her work. The courtship naturally failed, and later on, when the flirtation with the Irish girl fizzled out, he " went his way enjoying the prospect of a long respite from further love-making, and very far from realising the ineptitude with which he had conducted it."

It is all very well to smile at this now and say, " Good old G.B.S.," but imagine the reactions of the first forty publishers to whom *Immaturity* was offered, as they tried to make some sense out of this dexterous double-crossing. They may have been interested in the strange Irish stew, but they had their market to think about, and they knew with the certainty of British business men of the seventies, that the public did not want mutton, horns and hoofs on the one dish. It was bad enough to have several different kinds of lovemaking in a book, and to poke fun at all of them, but there was worse : beneath the most ordinary incidents in the most sedate places there was a continuous play of sly stabs and jeers at a social stratification which every English writer of the day accepted as his frame of reference. It was not that these writers were dull or timid, or particularly pious. Swinburne's whipped cream lyrics were making the under-graduates dizzy, Meredith was writing *The Egoist*,

and R. L. S. was travelling with a donkey in the
Cevennes in 1878 ; Arnold and Tennyson were sleek
enough perhaps, but Carlyle and Butler were not;
Hardy, Eliot, Trollope, and Reade were writing
at the top of their form ; there was plenty of variety
and plenty of criticism, subtle and otherwise, and all
kinds of authors, including Ouida and Mayne Reid,
could find a market, on one condition. They must
always make dukes talk like dukes, and coachmen
behave like coachmen. They might, and did, make
earls fall in love with dressmakers, but the dressmaker must know her place. The earl might be
brutal or beneficent, but not in one book and under
the same name. Every character had to be true to
type and the types to be clearly defined ; literary
matter had to have a firm British background to be
marketable. Even *Erewhon* (1872) and *The Egoist*
(1879) filled this bill. For the strength of Butler's
satire came in the first place from his intensely
English classical education, and Meredith hid *his*
onslaught under cover of the English landscape,
spacious parks, cherry blossoms and fine wine.

It was all very well for a finished craftsman to
pass off one anomaly decked out with the usual
furnishings, and surrounded by footmen and fashionable figures, but it was another thing for an unknown
to offer the publishers a book full of Sir Willoughbys
in the raw. There was a good market for moralising,
however awkward, or for ingenious impiety, or for
almost any kind of writing on artistic matters, but

there was none for a novel in which introspection and motive analysis played about the actions of every single character and made tatters of the story. Shaw couldn't see the play for the actors. He couldn't allow his people to take a step without calling attention to the muscle contraction which made it possible, and he would turn aside from their clothes and carriages on the slightest excuse, to skin them alive and probe for nerves. He did not know how to use his gift with moderation, and his book was like nothing on earth.

He scarcely understood how strange and vaguely disturbing was this dissecting-room style. He had known all along that it was an extraordinary thing to be alive, but he was only beginning to find that it was mighty awkward as well—for he did not seem to fit. There were so many lovely things to feel and so many delightful things to think about, but no one else seemed to bother with them, or even to notice they were there. The others seemed to be like him—they had bodies and faces, and two feet and so on—but inside they were different. They had ears, for instance, and they couldn't hear. Music hardly seemed to affect them at all, and they were able to tolerate dreadful performances and even to murmur lying appreciations of them. It was difficult to make any kind of contact with these people, for when asked some perfectly simple question about themselves, they were offended and turned away, or else looked at him as if he had said something indecent. He spoke English, yet he was unable to get into communication with them. There was some kind of a rush going on, which was deeply concerned with food and clothes, shops and ships, shares and banks. He was no dreamer (he says he was, but don't mind him), he saw the use of all these things as clearly as you do, but he was perfectly sure that they were not what he wanted. As he said to his friend Harriet, " Suppose you enjoy yourself more in keeping out of the rush than scrambling in it ? " Robert Smith was always putting up questions like that—not as concealed assertions but as genuine " Why nots " demanding sensible answers—and the questions cut across the very core of the conventions which held the 1870's together.

He was asking them not as a philosopher or sociologist, but as a matter of immediate and intimate interest to his author, who wanted to know what he was for, and whether there was any reason why he should do one thing more than another. If he enjoyed watching, why should he work ? If he enjoyed one particular kind of activity, why should he undertake another ? He must have been told by everyone, " Because there's no money in it," but that was no use. He wasn't asking " Where is money ? " but " Why are men ? " There must be some reason for them—or was life unreasonable ? He was prepared to consider that, for purposes of argument, but privately this was the one point on which Bernard was obstinate and intolerant. On everything else he had an open mind, but, by God, if the world wasn't reasonable it had better look out. He would lick it into shape if he had to do it single-handed. That German might try to get people to lie down and die, but this young sprig of an Irishman was going to stand up and live; he wouldn't say die while grass grew or water ran.

Immaturity was rejected unanimously, but that didn't matter. He was twenty-three and able to see through everything and everybody. There was a fascination about writing; he enjoyed creating characters, giving them their heads for a few pages, and then taking them apart. The writing of his first book had only whetted his appetite. It had taught him many things; among others that he could not make a novel by following his fancy all over the place. He must get some central idea and stick to it. His second novel, *The Irrational Knot*, was the result. It is a study of mating and marriage seen through the eyes of a two-fisted Irish-American named Edward Connolly. The shy, tentative Smith with his Peter Pannish charm vanishes, and this new hero comes on, with his jaw set, to study the manœuvres of Man and Woman in three modes. He starts one hundred per cent materialist, telling all the other characters one by one where they get off. The book is like the first in its isolation of individuals from one another and from a background. Everyone is considered by himself and on his own merits. There are no principles, only pictures of people and events. There is a central theme but no central theory. And there is far too much microscope. Connolly knows too much. Even his creator can't stand such a god-almighty man for four hundred pages, and gets a woman to give him a trimming about page 250. Towards the end he softens mysteriously, and the downright determinism begins to curl up at the edges. He begins to murmur to himself, "I am for the fullest attainable life," and to have his doubts about "Liberty." George Bernard had got tired of rationalistic analysis and snapshotting. It did not get him anywhere. It gave him a sense of power for a time, and it was fun to drop Connolly into the middle of an 1880 drawing-room and watch him blow up, but that was not enough.

He was no farther forward after writing two books. He had tried the discursive method with Bernard in the lead, and he had tried the crowbar method with George throwing his weight about, but neither satisfied him. He felt as important as ever, but he couldn't get started. His conscience would not let him settle down to work and help to support his mother and sister. He had turned matters over thoroughly in 300,000 carefully written words ; he had read nearly all the books in the British Museum, and he had observed people in and out of doors with the greatest attention ; and he asked himself why they were all going on like this after umpteen million years. It was incredible, it was maddeningly mysterious. it was wildly funny—for they were all so concerned about trifles—so carried off their feet with their love-fancies. He saw through all those. They were just a trick which kept the show going on, and what was the use of keeping it going if it didn't mean anything. Perhaps the German was right. No, to hell with him ! Life was for good, it must be for beauty too. There was a clue here, dim and elusive, but worth following. And when he saw anything worth following he followed it promptly and for all he was worth.

Music, painting, poetry, were the best things. They were permanent beauty caught and crystallised out of life. They were the only thing worth while. So his next book was *Love among the Artists*. There is no need to follow him through it to *Cashel Byron's Profession*, written in 1882, and on to *The Unsocial Socialist*, his last attempt at novel writing, completed in 1883 ; for after 1881 genuine free thinking slackened, and the outlines of the new creed began to appear. He went on writing all this time apparently without the slightest hope of publication. He began *Immaturity* about 1877 and finished his fifth book in 1883. Nearly a million words and not one carelessly written sentence ! It was a wonderful apprenticeship. It was no mere mechanical training, but an orgie of furious thinking, at least up to 1883. After that there was no more speculative thought but only more and more furious propaganda.

95

From this time Art was his religion, and Shelley was its prophet. *He* had that "intuitive perception of the underlying analogies, the secret subterranean passages between matter and soul" which transcend scientific thinking. Men like him—Blake, Goethe, and the rest—could pluck out rich glowing meanings from the heart of labouring Nature and create new truth. Man's destiny was to go upward from plane to plane of knowledge through greater and greater appreciation of beauty. And the great ones of the world were the creative artists who could hew out fresh models from this amorphous world which was surging aimlessly at the mercy of itself and had only man to rely on for further progress. Some such ideas had been floating in the upper intellectual airs of Europe for a century. They had drifted north from France, and come to earth in the German universities. Soon they were spreading out to fire young imaginations and fuse themselves into the work of the artists of all countries. Wagner was caught by them. There had been a riot in Paris in 1861 over *Tannhäuser*—for the professional critics made trouble at first—but 1876 saw the *Ring* at Bayreuth and in 1880 the new operas were startling and fascinating listeners by the thousand. He was winning everywhere, and his theories, his genius and his themes swept young Shaw off his feet and whirled him into the twentieth century waving the banner of Creative Evolution.

But not quite. It will not do to rush things like

this. Perhaps in another thousand years, when the half century 1880 to 1930 looks like a passing hour, it may be possible to compress Wagner and Shaw into a sentence or two, and see clearly how much of the thought of nineteenth-century England was made in Germany. Just now it is enough to know that this new drama with its blend of sound, words, movement and scene, into one harmonic whole, was a revelation to the young listener tuned to perfection for appreciation of just such a display.

It was clear that art was all-important, and that artists were the salt of the earth, but that was not enough. Shaw never had much use for generalities. He needed something definite, concrete, and personal, and it was here that Samuel Butler and the life cell came in. Butler was a man who had been in and out of the Church of England as Shaw had been in and out of the Church of Ireland, except that Butler had been in longer and deeper. Like Shaw too, he had a devouring passion for order and honour, and was intensely sensitive to the oddities of human conduct. He was full of the evolutionary spirit of the times, and was being tripped up at every point by the non-negotiability of the results of a classical education, just as Shaw was being harassed by his failure to sell his artistic knowledge. He had gone to New Zealand to try to make a living, and he had come home to try to teach the English people how to live. He was not satisfied with Darwin ; he felt that man could not live on rocks alone, however rich their record, and he wanted to prove this to the public. He had a remarkable gift of expressing himself in clean, lean English. When he sighted hypocrisy he was swift and ruthless as a greyhound.

Butler was fascinated by the life cell. Lenses had improved, and the foundations of cytology were being laid in Germany. In 1861 the cell was defined as " a small mass of protoplasm endowed with the attributes of life." That was fine ; delight greeted the discovery that there were two simple ultimates from which the inorganic and organic worlds were built up. The millions of years of the geologists and the billions of miles of the astronomers had been hard to bear, but now that it was known that everything was made from such teeny-weeny bits, everyone was reassured. The only thing that remained was to find a formula for the cell. It was here that Butler jibbed, for he didn't want it to have a formula ; he loved the simple cell, and its way of dividing up and yet remaining itself, so that it seemed to live for ever. He read more and more about it, and seemed to see clearly how the cell by striving, developed itself and passed these developments to its offspring. He became its champion, and defended it against all comers. The cell was, in its own way, an individual, and must not be treated as a tiny machine. It had a will and a memory ; otherwise how could it adapt itself so well to outside changes, and pass on good habits to its children. That

Will was the essence of life. It was a Sacred Mystery;
and Butler rapped the knuckles of every pawing
materialist that tried to lay a hand on it. Further-
more, this elemental unit of life had learned to
assemble itself in masses, some of which had charming habits, like a rose-bush, and others shocking
habits, like a tiger. Further up the scale came
Homer and further still Handel. The cell, with its
urge and its wonderful assembly of habits, had made
man that man might create higher and still higher
forms of beauty, and the emotions and sense of
importance which man felt rising within him were
the cell's message to him from the past, and its own
mystic urge towards the future.

Butler's teaching was the link which Shaw needed
to bind together what he saw without and felt within.
But he did not take over Butler or Wagner without
question, any more than he took over Herder or
Goethe or Schopenhauer without looking them coolly
in the eye as who should say, " I'm Bernard Shaw
from Dublin, and this is the year 1882. If I can't
improve on you, I have no cellular tissue." If there
was anything worthwhile in this cell business (and
Bernard had his doubts), and in this warning within
to take himself seriously, it was that he must not
rest content with what others had done, but jump
right into the middle of things and *act*.

The world must be made fit for artists to work in.
There was no use writing novels, or composing
operas, or making beautiful things, when the world

H 2

did its best to starve those who made them. He had
real fellow-feeling with Wagner and Butler here, for
his fourth novel came back from the publishers just
as regularly as the others. But he didn't weep over
himself. In fact, by this time it looks as though he
had almost lost sight of himself in his concern for
Art and the Artists who were to come.

When after about five years in London he began
to take an active interest in the social organisation
about him, he found that he was not the only one
who objected to its petrified stratification, and that
from all angles men and women were coming
together to fight. They did not know what they
were up against, or how to tackle it, and they
were making the wildest attacks on people and
things without any plan whatever. Bradlaugh was
one focus; Hyndman was another; he had met
Marx, swallowed him whole, and produced a
pamphlet called *England for All* in 1881. William
Morris didn't have to read anything; he wasn't
like the bookworms, he was a manual worker, and
he knew without reading. He just *knew*. He didn't
require statistics or philosophy to tell him that
England was in a mess. He was a simple man
and he wanted a simple cure like a huge hose or
a big bomb. There were others linked with
Hyndman and Morris in the Democratic Federation
in 1883, and all were in perfect agreement about
everything, except what they wanted and the way
to get it. In no time at all there was a fine old split,

and Morris budded off in a separate Socialist League. By 1884 English Socialism was going ahead wildly in all directions, and proving nothing except that it was very difficult to get a group of free-thinking Englishmen to work together for any length of time, for any purpose whatever.

The intellectuals had tried to combine with the miners and dockers to make a way of escape from ugliness and starvation, and they found themselves getting on one another's nerves. Even the arrangement of meetings and the selection of speakers gave trouble. Fresh young newcomers were eager to pick holes in any policy that was more than a month old, and were confident that the better a man was dressed the greater and wiser he was. Later on Shaw said, " the combination of the petulant rich man with the ignorant poor one is perhaps the most desperately unworkable on the political chessboard." It is easy to see this in retrospect. The remarkable thing is that he could see it at the time, and threw in his lot from the very beginning with the first group to become effective and to force the pace. He was a live member of the Fabian Society from its formation in 1884. He came into the middle of that struggling, milling mass of uplifters—a raw youth without a particle of experience of politics, committee work or propaganda—saw clearly what was wrong, and steered himself straight into the best position for the purpose he had in view. It was a triumph for the habit of meditation, observation, and more meditation. He had lived in seclusion for years; he had fastened on two points, one an assumption and the other an intuition; and henceforward he followed them wherever they led him with Euclidean rationality and Cromwellian zeal. For eight years the world had tried to flatten him out, and had then suddenly turned and handed him the Fabian Society —a toy for his delight.

CHAPTER V

HE had been in the wilderness for six years—there
is no more desolate place in the world than London
for a sensitive young man who doesn't like it and
won't give in.   Till 1882 he never questioned the
permanence of the social structure about him, not
even when he was poking his fingers through its ribs.
He girded against the æsthetic ignorance of the rich,
but he accepted them as he accepted bad weather.
He saw that money could always be made by
certain cunning activities, but it did not seem that
this could be changed any more than that the
Thames could be made to run uphill.   Some men
were greedy and got rich as bladders filled, others
weren't money-tight and stayed poor as sieves
leaked, and that was all there was to it.   The forces
which produced riches and poverty were all part
of a regardless and unalterable environment.

One day—September 5th, 1882—his curiosity
brought him to hear Henry George lecturing on
Land and Rent, and he suddenly saw past the people
into the system about him.   He saw, of course, in
his own way.   That is to say, in a very simple,
fiercely analytical, terrifically honest way.   And he
reacted as usual by immediate action.   He had been

seeing through people for years, now he suddenly saw through the system. It was as though a vision had suddenly appeared in a bank of fog—or rather as if the world of men and property had turned into a sketch-book, in which all the pictures told the same jerky little story :

All wealth from land,
All rent from wealth,
　　Property is theft.

The tenant works but doesn't own,
The landlord owns but doesn't work,
　　Property is theft.

The more the men,
The less the land,
The richer the landlord,
The poorer the rest,
　　Property is theft.

He had been ill at ease in the City, but he had assumed that London was inevitable and that he had no choice between going on being unhappy, or selling himself cheap and joining in the scramble. Now he found that London was not a natural product, but an artificial institution—in fact, a den of thieves. He had been right all along in holding out against it. His intuition has not misled him. His confusions and uncertainties were suddenly resolved by this new analysis ; all his dislikes and longings, all his experiences in the Dublin estate office suddenly coalesced about the phrase " Property is theft," and London blazed in a new and lurid light. It was the core of a lying world. His ill-ease disappeared in a flash before the idea that the environment could be changed. He was filled with tingling conviction. It was right to fight.

It was characteristic of him to realise that all his knowledge was useless till he knew more of economics. He came away from that Progress and Poverty meeting, and settled down to read Marx and study economics, as an ambitious artist studies anatomy. It is well to note here that this sudden change of activity was no abnormal break, but a perfectly natural branching off from the stem of his main interest. But it will be easier to make the events of the next period clear if he is seen as a sort of super-skater cutting on a mighty scale two loops which look separate at first but are finally seen to form a single expert figure eight. One loop was the New Politics and the other the New Protestantism. One was centred in the Fabian Society and the other in the Theatre. They spread out in ever-increasing sweeps, encircling the world from Moscow to Mexico, and New York to London. Each is interesting in itself, but puzzling without the other. Points of inflexion don't interest whole-time socialists or playgoers, and to them he always appears to be going off at a tangent when he is really linking his double roles with the smoothest dexterity.

The two roles must be examined separately and at some length and when this is done, as in the pages

which follow, it will be clear why the laughs sometimes stop in the stalls and start in the gallery.

Reading *Capital* was slow work. There was no
English edition, and young Shaw had to plough
through the French version, following that amazing
argument as best he could. Even in English it is
not easy to read Marx but there are compensations.
His argument piles up layer on layer and the reader
has at first the despairing sensation of being crushed
under sheer weight of word-jugglery ; and then
suddenly he is revived by a word-picture so crisp and
vigorous that he feels the book would have been an
even greater success as an anti-capitalistic tract if
the attempts at logic had been left out. Marx is like
A. A. Milne's cricketing postman who had two
deliveries—one in the morning with correspondence,
and the other in the afternoon with leg breaks.

Take this, for instance :

> In order to discover how the elementary
> expression of the value of a commodity lies
> hidden in the value relation of two commodities,
> we must in the first place consider the latter
> entirely apart from its quantitative aspect. The
> usual mode of procedure is generally the reverse,
> and in the value relation nothing is seen but the
> proportion between definite quantities of two
> different sorts of commodities that are considered
> equal to one another. It is apt to be forgotten
> that the magnitudes of different things can be
> compared quantitatively only when these magni-

tudes are expressed in terms of the same unit. It is only as expressions of such a unit that they are of the same denomination and therefore commensurable.

and compare it with :

One fine morning in the year 1836, Nassau W. Senior, who may be called the *bel esprit* of English economists, well known alike for his economical "science" and his beautiful style, was summoned from Oxford to Manchester to learn in the latter place the political economy that he taught in the former. The manufacturers elected him as their champion, not only against the newly passed Factory Act, but against the more menacing ten hours agitation. With their usual practical acuteness, they had found out that the learned Professor "wanted a good deal of finishing," and it was this discovery that caused them to write for him.

or read this :

The price form, however, is not only compatible with the possibility of a quantitative incongruity between magnitude of value and price, *i.e.*, between the former and its expression in money, but it may also conceal a qualitative inconsistency, so much so, that although money is nothing but the value form of commodities, price ceases altogether to express value.

and then this :

107

The new machine-hands are exclusively girls and young women. With the help of mechanical force they destroy the monopoly which male labour had of the heavier work, and they drive off from the lighter work numbers of old women and very young children. The overpowering competition crushes the weakest of the manual labourers. The fearful increase in death from starvation during the last ten years in London runs parallel with the extension of machine sewing.

and try to imagine what the first volume of *Capital* is like. Marx couldn't touch a general idea without doing five pages of German minuet about it, but when he got a fact, he was like a smith at an anvil. Shaw, as will be seen, was not impressed by the minuets, but he must have been delighted with Nassau W. Senior's trip to Manchester. Also he probably liked the scientific flavour of :

the body as an organic whole is more easy of study than are the cells of that body. In the analysis of economic forms, moreover, neither microscope nor chemical reagents are of use. The force of abstraction must replace both. But in bourgeois society, the commodity form of the product of labour—or the value form of the commodity—is the economic cell form.

Which brings Marx into line with Butler. But—and this is a most remarkable " but "—he didn't swallow the labour theory of value like Hyndman and the rest. Marx had managed to stamp it into them by arguments so abstruse and Hegelian that it seemed blasphemous to question them. He knew the value of slogans, and when, after two hundred repetitions of the words " surplus value," he said, " capital is congealed labour," they all repeated it reverently after him.

Shaw never minded a little breezy blasphemy in a good cause, and in due time he said Marx was wrong. He presented his case against the labour theory of value jocularly at first in the hope of provoking a discussion which would clear the air. To his astonishment, he found that the English Socialist leaders could not refute his criticism, and worse, could not even see that their failure to do so would be fatal in the long run. Their eyes were fixed partly on particular abuses, partly on Marx, and partly on themselves. They had no time to waste on theories. He was different ; he hated being fooled as much as he hated fooling himself, and he set out single-handed to find a theory of value which would stand up to facts.

He soon found himself in strange and difficult country, but nothing could stop him. He was heroic. Even when, on his search for new light on " value " he found Jevons reducing it to $y = f(x)$ and $y.dx = du$, he was unstaggered. He bought a text-book and started a new study. He had never cared about algebra ; in his schooldays it had seemed to him a treacherous subject which enticed the student away from the solid ground of concrete fact, from real numbers of miles and pints and shillings to a region of terrible uncertainty where a might be anything and x was unknown. He was all for clear-cut issues, numerical relationships and tangible classifications. When someone said $ax^2 + bx + c = 0$, he suspected trickery; He couldn't stand the man who furtively slips $\sqrt{-1}$ into an equation as a poacher slips a ferret into a rabbit hole. He was badly fitted to deal with problems involving functions and rates, but he went after them in that wholehearted magnificent way which was the glory of his youth.

The differentials defeated him, but there was something attractive about the Jevons theory, and he struggled on till he had absorbed enough of it to satisfy him. The relative merits of different value theories do not matter here; it is only his way with them that is to be noted—his realisation of the need for sound foundation, and his willingness to undertake any kind of gruelling work to try and find them. The people about him seemed to be content to have at their disposal two such lovely words for platform purposes as " bourgeoisie " and " proletariat," and did not understand his passion for getting down to the roots. Shaw saw from the beginning the need for going back to first principles, and his own difficulties with them taught him something of the complexity of economics. They also showed him what his role in the struggle was to be. He saw on one side a mass of well-meaning ignorance, and, on the other, a mass of unconscious stupidity, and he decided that he must brush up both, and introduce them. He must be a teacher. He knew, as no other Socialist did, how much there was to learn, and he was full of that restless energy which had driven him out of Dublin and through five unpublished novels.

He knew that he must learn, and here again he showed that genius and common sense are inseparable. For there are two ways of getting knowledge ; one is to dig it out with much toil, and the other is to find a friend who has done the digging. The friend in this case was Sidney Webb, whose fortune it was in those days to be in the very chart-room of state finance, and whose faculties were such that he could do all the digging needed without getting his hands blistered. In fact, he enjoyed it, and could cover as much ground in a week with pleasure as other men might slave over painfully and unprofitably for a year. He knew all about dividends, companies, costing, capital appreciation, unearned incomes, property valuation, and rent, in a way no ordinary member of the public understands; he knew them as a washerwoman knows a shirt, he knew them inside out—he was in the Income Tax office. He was one of the brightest young men in the best civil service in the world ; he probably first got his eye on assessment returns in the mass about 1879, and by 1881, when he was transferred to the Colonial Office, the most intimate and curious transactions of the property-owning and business world of London were an open book to him.

Sidney Webb had scarcely begun hearing financial confessions when Shaw first saw him. It was at a small meeting of the sort attended by earnest young men in the eighties, and the proceedings must have been dull enough. The ordinary audience noticed that one of the speakers was more convincing than the others but Shaw noticed the same thing in his own special way. He noticed that Webb knew exactly what he was talking about, that he held in reserve a mighty mass of knowledge, that he picked out just what he required, packed it up in a neat sentence, and discharged it to produce exactly the effect he desired. He had no use for oratory, he simply stated his case in a neat, impersonal, efficient, unemotional way ; he was clear-headed, he was full of facts, he was sincere ; he was irresistible to the young Irishman who had been searching London for a sensible man for six years. Webb's way of approach to the problem of poverty had been *viâ* history—John Stuart Mill—and more history, particularly the history of England. He knew it complete with footnotes. He could say offhand—" the Corporation of London actually carried on the business of fire insurance from 1681 to 1683 "—to the discomfort of City men who tried to show that his ideas were new-fangled and impractical. His civil service work on top of his reading had made history alive for him. He saw the events of the past in terms of social groupings, grab, political rivalry, and ignorant attempts at regulation. He saw in his experience from day to day the raw material for the history of the future, and he was searching for some way to make that history neater than the history of the past.

Shaw knew from the first that Webb was his man. Whether Webb knew Shaw's value is doubtful. He had reached a dignified position in the Colonial Office by 1882, and he was really very English. It is most unlikely that he would have been attracted by a man with a brogue who was a walking indiscretion. Did Shaw put on a silk hat and an upper-class manner, and talk like a higher executive officer, or did he dance off like a will-o'-the-wisp spirit of democracy, drawing the other after him in sober steps with his uncanny, coaxing piping or what? It is better that the truth should not be known—it's more fun to keep on guessing. Anyhow, the Fabian Society was the result.

They entered as members, but in a few years the society belonged to them. Webb's knowledge and policy dominated it. He had made a synthesis of Mill, evolution and his reading of history. He saw England—the British Constitution—the British Isles —the British Empire—as a mighty growth within which was quickening with the centuries the great Spirit of Democracy. He saw the spirit emerging with time into definite forms, heedless of the interests of individual leaders and political parties. He felt

that there was a Great Purpose to be served and
that in the nineteenth century the rulers of the State
should make themselves conscious of it, and act in
accordance with " the great sweep of social tenden-
cies," instead of struggling in petty rivalry and
stupid ambition. He saw how states and cities had
by degrees and almost unwittingly taken over
one service and industry after another—the
management of the Church, the details of public
worship, the building of ships and houses, the
provision of gasworks, and upkeep of roads and
bridges. He saw how this communisation had
spread to the colonies and how the central authorities
there had built railways and theatres and become
dealers in guano and quinine. He saw all these
things, and a thousand others, with that vividness
which comes from direct experience. He learnt
from his books what had happened, and he knew
from his daily work what was happening. He saw
how the State gathered its income, and how, in
recent years, it had been forced to dip deeper and
deeper into the pockets of the rich to provide better
facilities for the population as a whole. He saw,
moreover, how interdependent were all public and
private activities and tastes, and knew how the sheep-
men of New Zealand swore as the ladies of London
changed from flannel to *crêpe de chine*. He saw that
the British Empire had become by degrees a huge
co-operative business without knowing it. He had
a vision of underlying meanings and ultimate

purposes, and on one occasion he even said : " the life of the community transcends that of its individual members," but generally he was patient and practical, and looked for ways and means rather than for beginnings and ends. The big Co-op.— the British Empire—seemed to him hopelessly disorganised, owing to the stupidity of the political leaders who were " so near to the individual events, that they were blind to the onward sweep of the column," and owing still more to the greed and laziness of the capitalists and landlords who lived by respectable forms of slavery and robbery.

He wanted others to see the truth as he saw it, but he realised that it was only those of higher intellectual gifts that were capable of seeing the Social Organism as a whole, and devoting themselves to its service. The rest must be taught carefully and gradually, and the Fabians must learn in order to teach. There must be a science of society as there were sciences of stars, rocks, and plants, and man must set himself to make it, as those other sciences were made, by collecting, grouping, classifying and summarising social facts, till at last the laws which governed it would be as familiar as the laws of motion. This was the long view for those, who, like himself, had the faith and patience to undertake weary statistical work which might not bear full fruit for centuries. But there was also immediate work to be done and every statutory authority could do its share. Each council and corporation had powers ready for use in the general social good, if only it could be persuaded to use them. If Socialists could be elected on these bodies and to Parliament, so much the better. But if not, then Conservatives, Liberals, and Independents were to be approached and persuaded to do something communistic. That word need not be used, but they could be urged to put up a pump, abolish a toll bridge, build a library, or, best of all, become landlords on a grand scale with huge housing schemes. Fabians must not be snobs ; it must not be beneath them to persuade a duke to attend the House of Lords to vote for a national drainage scheme, which would improve the value of his land. The duke would generally be bright enough to see that this was a Desirable Improvement, even if he could not foresee that his son might have to sell the improved land to the State for public parks, owing to heavy death duties and higher income tax which would be imposed to pay for the drainage. It took four or five years of discussion and experiment to work out this policy of steady pressure and penetration, but eventually it became the basis of all Fabian activity. Slowly, gradually, inevitably, that was how the Life Force has created the world, and man must conform. He must take for his motto " the inevitability of gradualness," and learn to serve.

In the Fabian Society Webb had the science, but it was Shaw that had the punch and his colleagues were quick to realise it. He must at first have seemed a very odd person to William Clarke from Cambridge and Graham Wallas from Oxford. His tutors had been of a type scarcely known at either place, and his special branch of research had not been of late looked on kindly by those in charge of English Universities. But he was in congenial company and his charm was irresistible ; his power of incisive analysis of human conduct was a magnet to minds running in conventional English grooves. Webb could take a Department of State apart, as a watchmaker opens a watch ; and he could show how it was wound up every year by the Ministry of Finance, how some parts worked, and others were ornamental. But Shaw could take a man apart and show with vivid wit the curious underground passages linking his wishes, words and actions. He had developed his natural gift by years of meditation and novel writing, and after a short period of intimacy with Sidney Webb and the other economists, with whom his interests brought him in contact, he was ready for political action.

He had the true missionary spirit, and he began by preaching. The reactions following that first revelation by Henry George never left him, and he was prepared to do anything to spread the light which burned so brightly within him. He understood better than any other Fabian how to spread it ; he knew the plain man, and knew that he could only appeal to him in the simplest terms with concrete instances and short, crisp sentences. His own difficulties in mastering economic principles helped him here. To make things clear to himself, he thought in terms of real fields and real men. He didn't care about slippery thinking-counters like " commodities," he preferred to deal with cabbages, barley, furniture and fire-irons. So it was that when he could get even a dozen people gathered together in the street, all the farmers' sons, carpenters and blacksmiths understood exactly what he was saying ; he presented his case in a form which they could take home with them. He was a wonderful teacher. He was full of his subject and a master of language ; he had a voice like gold, and knew exactly how to use it. He had found out at last what to do with George Bernard Shaw, and he was doing it with his whole heart and his whole mind, and with all his faculties. His musical ear, his wit, his richly stored imagination, were all pressed into service in the most wonderful exhibition of public speaking ever staged as a free show in London. He was launched on his life's work at last after that long stretch of solitude and rejection ; how he must have enjoyed himself in the next twenty years as he spoke and wrote and raged to advance the cause of Socialism ! The precision, the gusto, the extravagance, the sheer whirlwind energy of those early onslaughts on the existing organisation of society saturate his first Fabian Essays, written in 1888. They were published with others in 1889, with a warning preface that—" There are at present no authoritative teachers of Socialism. The essayists make no claim to be more than communicative learners," but that must have been just Webb's fun. On September 7th, 1888, Shaw was telling the British Association members at Bath that " the militant organisation of the working classes and general insurrection—remains the only finally possible alternative to the Social Democratic Programme which I have sketched to-day."

But, sure as he was of himself and of the programme, there was one thing that bothered him. In those days a refined anarchism was fashionable. Prince Kropotkin had made it respectable in Europe and it flourished in cultured quarters in Boston, Mass. Anarchists were inclined to flutter jealously on the borders of socialistic organisations. They could not come in, because combination was against their principles, and they daren't stay out, because the Socialists claimed to be the leading champions of freedom and the modern champions of the rights of man. No self-respecting anarchist could tolerate such a claim from men who were sinking their individuality in a communistic pool, and offering themselves up trussed and gagged to a State idol called the Social Organism. Pure and high-spirited anarchists joined with the social democrats in calling down fire from heaven on slum landlords, Stock Exchange sharks, and all the sweaters and grinders of the poor, but when Webb and Co. tried to persuade them to get together and do something, they rose up in all their outraged, individual divinity, and refused to submit to the discipline involved in any form of association whatever. It was a real difficulty. Webb wanted Justice, the others wanted Liberty, and the gods wouldn't kiss. The logicians said that there was nothing for it but to build two temples and put one god in each, but Shaw would have none of this. He understood both sides only too well, for George was all for Social Democracy, and Bernard knew that the anarchists were right. In fact, it was because he realised, better than anyone about him, the difficulties in which an honourable man lands himself when he makes private judgment the final court of appeal, that he became a special pleader against the ultra-individualists. He saw that this was no new dispute and that the rival high priests would multiply and destroy one another. He saw that socialistic solidarity must be preserved at all costs in face of the common enemy if any constructive work was to be done, and he spent much precious time in those early struggling years of the Fabian Society trying to keep the high-minded from being hasty.

His lecture-essay on the "Impossibilities of Anarchism" is a masterpiece. He doesn't quite dodge the issue, but takes care not to face it long enough to start trouble. He gives a page or so to principles, and then in a masterly way brings the trouble-makers down to practical things—economic measures—ways and means—brass tacks. He persuades them to come off their high horses and take a look at things like bread, farms, houses, and income tax ; in ten pages he has them spellbound with the simplicity and inevitability of Fabianism ; in twenty he has them agreeing that " there is no natural liberty but only natural law remorselessly enforced," and that the only hope of salvation from the eternal tyranny of Nature lies in the establishment of Social Democracy. And finally he manages to convey the impression that the most earnest anarchist in his audience is a lukewarm stick-in-the-mud, that Bakunin and the bomb-throwers are mere babes in thirst for destruction and hatred of the tyranny of authority, compared with G. B. Shaw. You can almost hear the splintering explosions and see the twisted bodies as he speaks of the policemen and the soldiers, the parsons and the plutocrats, of the existing system. Yet there is not a word of encouragement for Anarchism, nor a sentence of incitement, in that bloodthirsty peroration which sent the Kropotkin disciples home with an uneasy feeling that Fabianism was perhaps a very subtle and advanced form of anarchism. He was not, as will be seen, quite comfortable in his own mind about the problem raised, but he was so sweetly reasonable and generally outrageous that all budding anarchists danced to his piping, and followed him down the Fabian lane.

He was from the beginning the practical clarifier and conciliator. Webb's idea of slow, resistless, social action like the weathering of rocks or the growing of grass appealed to him immensely. It was in keeping with the ancient tradition of the landed Shaws of Kilkenny, and yet in touch with the latest scientific thought—or what was called the Modern Spirit. There was a wonderful sense of power in seeing the world making itself, in watching it grow, and knowing that one was called to lend a hand. He felt that few had such vision, as he saw men stumbling about confusedly, and using their vital forces in quarrelling instead of co-operating. It was his mission in the political field to be a mediator as well as a teacher, and to show the means by which all could work together to create a better world. Such uppish convictions would have ruined him had he taken them altogether seriously. He accepted them—but with considerable amusement. Beneath his absorption with socialism and his Fabian associations, he remained always the observer—the recorder—the artist-comedian. He was the most loyal of colleagues, but he couldn't help seeing that his fellow socialists were men and women before they were anything else ; they had many childish ways, and it was necessary to use a good deal of tact to get them to work together. In some ways during the twenty years from 1884–1904 he was like a very capable mother of a large and troublesome family, chaffing and coaxing to get the day's work done, and not afraid to do some spanking when necessary.

He was a grand worker and he finished up that score of breathless years as Vestryman and Borough Councillor for St. Pancras for the term 1897–1903. He took his share of the load wherever he found it, and he practised his preaching in the council chamber and committee room for a full term. It seems an anti-climax for the boy novelist and the flaming orator to settle down to that dreary grind of public business with minutes, resolutions and manœuvres about officials' salaries taking up so much valuable time, but he went through it like an apprentice learning a useful trade, and his later writings are full of the ballast of the knowledge of local government and the machinery of adminis-tration gained in those six municipal years.

He was wildly busy in other fields all this time. He was writing startling plays at a furious rate with one hand, and superlative dramatic criticism for the *Saturday Review* with the other; he was having the plays published, rehearsed and produced; he was getting married; he was furiously engaged in every form of socialistic activity that a super-charged ingenuity could devise; and in his spare time he was learning to ride the bicycle.

There had been bicycles before, but this was the " safety," and it was making a stir that no one born after 1890 can understand. How can it be described to a generation that tries a motor cycle, a speedboat, a sports car and a monoplane before it is twenty, and then looks round wearily for something newer and faster. They didn't get bored so quickly in the 'nineties. Magazines were full of stories of the new swift method of travel. H. G. Wells made a romance about a cycling clerk. Any young woman could get a name for being an advanced thinker or a shameless hussy by riding a bicycle in public; correct young men averted their eyes as she passed. Sunday cycling was a sin. Tempers were lost and families disrupted about "bloomers"—called "rational costume" in honour of Herbert Spencer. It is hard to believe that there are still millions of men and women in England who lived through all this and whose hearts thrill to the tune of *Daisy Bell;* and harder still to believe that Shaw at forty was only just getting expert at ripping downhill on his first bike, with his feet stuck on the fork rests and the pedals whirling madly beneath him.

He was able to buy his own bicycles by 1896. He began, as a journalist, to help his mother and sister to keep a roof over their heads, about 1885. He never seems to have realised his possibilities in this field till friends like William Archer and Annie Besant, not deceived by his air of being a young man of independent means, who wore frayed cuffs as a fad, inveigled him into it. Once launched on the staff of the *World* in 1886 he knew that journalistic criticism of art and artists was his natural trade. From 1886 to 1898 he was reviewer and art critic to the *Pall Mall Gazette, World, Star* and *Saturday Review* in succession; that is, he was supposed to write from week to week something about a book, picture, exhibition, concert or play of public interest at the moment. That was how critics earned their living ; they wrote carefully arranged bits of praise and depreciation of certain features of the work presented to them, and let it go at that. Above all things they avoided personal feeling, or any suggestion that the writer, painter, singer or actor was a human being. Artists were supposed to turn out their work as a lathe turns out a bolt, and certain approved standards were applied like calipers to determine its quality. Ruskin, for instance, had decided the features which a painting must have to make it a good picture, and all that the art critic had to do was to learn the rules and go ahead with his column week by week.

Shaw changed all that—almost single-handed. He knew music, pictures, books, as a good groom knows horses. He didn't have to poke about for rules. His knowledge was sure, intimate, part of himself. He poured out criticism as a practised hostess pours out tea. He had grown up with those things, loved them, studied them, and he didn't have to speak about art, work, and workers, in a hushed voice with strange, stiff words. Even the newest work—if it had any good in it—was familiar in hundreds of old, everyday, interesting ways. He had only to read books or look at pictures, or listen to music, and then say what he thought about them as plainly, as clearly as he could. It was very readable, fresh, chatty, easy-going criticism, but it was most irregular. There was no special vocabulary used, no prescribed rules, and an awful tendency to drag the artist into the open and take off some of his fashionable well-creased clothes. Shaw seemed to want to get away from mannerisms, materials, and the particular work in hand, and down to the man, and what he thought, felt, had to say for himself. When he found an artist copying or turning out stuff mechanically, or putting himself in front of the music, he put down his pen and took up a tomahawk. It was great fun, and it looked so easy that imitators came into the field at once, with disastrous results. Readers thought it was a great joke : " That fellow Shaw—the Socialist, you know—is writing about music. He doesn't know *a thing* about it, but he's fearfully funny. Last week he actually *criticised* Paderewski—said his playing was hard on the audience, but harder on Schumann—Imagine ! "

There was not at first much evidence of any particular theory about art. He had served the proper apprenticeship for his position, and, like a good plumber or cook or accountant, he was able to take the normal features in his stride and concentrate on the unusual. It is just this economy of effort, this sense of penetrating and exact observation carried out with the greatest ease, which gives those early criticisms their wonderful quality. You feel that he is prepared even to this day to stand over

every word he said.   He did not make up a criticism,
but rather set free a flood of expression, which still
tingles with his delight in writing it, and his conviction that what he had to say was worth saying.   It
was his mission in the artistic field to attack bad
work, to help the artist, to teach the public what to
look for, to make them thoroughly ashamed of
themselves where necessary, and to give praise
where it was due.   He managed to do all this without being an insufferable prig, by some magic of his
own, and a mock comedy treatment which it is
quite impossible to describe :

As to the singing, there was a tenor who
was compendiously announced as " Signor
Rawner, who has created so great a sensation
in Italy," and who is undoubtedly capable of
making an indelible mark anywhere. I listened
expectantly for *Deserto sulla terra*, knowing that
if the sensationist were a fine artist, his inter-
pretation of its musical character would surround
it with illusion, making it come from among the
trees in the moonlight, soft, distant, melancholy,
haunting ; whereas, if he were the common or
Saffron Hill Manrico, he would at once display
his quality by a stentorian performance in the
wing, putting all his muscle and wind into a
final B flat (substituted for G), and storming
London with that one wrong note alone. My
suspense was short. Signor Rawner, knowing
nothing about the musical character of the

serenade, but feeling quite sure about the B flat, staked his all on it ; and a stupendous yell it was. It is said that he can sing D ; and though he mercifully refrained from actually doing so, I have not myself the smallest doubt that he could sing high F in the same fashion if he only tried hard enough (*Music in London*, Vol. I, p. 8).

He was always like that when artists threw the piece out of focus, to show off a speciality, and the more famous the artist the harder he hit. Listen to this about Bernhardt :

Take, for example, the end of the third act of this *Princesse Lointaine* which she selects as her opportunity for one of those displays of vehemence which are expected from her as part of the conventional Bernhardt exhibition. It is pure rant and nothing else. When once she begins to tear through her lines at the utmost pitch of her voice, she shows no further sense of what she is saying, and is unable to recover herself when in the final speech the feeling changes. As her physical endurance threatens to fail, she tears along the faster, and finally rushes off the stage in a forced frenzy. I do not deny that there is something very exciting in a blind whirlwind of roaring energy. I have seen working-class audiences spring to their feet and cheer madly for three minutes at it. But then the artist was Mr. John Burns who can give

Madame Bernhardt a start of several miles at that particular sort of effect, and beat her easily. And I am bound to say, in justice to Mr. Burns, that I have never seen him bring down the curtain in this fashion until the play was really over, or substitute the peroration for the business part of the speech, whereas Madame Bernhardt does deliberately substitute rant for the business of the play. (*Our Theatre in the 'Nineties*, Vol. I, p. 168.)

There is more in this than meets the eye. He was standing up for the rights of the dramatist and for intelligent acting, but that was not all. He was not satisfied with his special mission as art critic, and long before 1895, when that passage was written, he had laid out his plan of campaign for bringing the theatre into line with the evolutionary thought of the day and making the stage a pulpit for modern prophets. He had published *The Quintessence of Ibsenism* in 1890 ; his first play, *Widowers' Houses*, was performed in 1892 ; and he was on his way to public favour with the production of *Arms and the Man* in 1894. Everything was working out according to plan, and he was using his position as a critic to obtain a hearing for true artists who grew plays instead of constructing them. It was all fair and square, as open and above board as that criticism of Bernhardt. He wanted actors to do something more than give a performance and he spurred them on, in a way all his own, to make the very best of their powers. But over and above that, he wanted them to fit and dovetail into a policy which had the same relation to the Great Purpose on the dramatic front as Fabianism in the political front. He wanted more of Ibsen's plays in London. The Social Organism was struggling on many fronts, using all kinds of men as weapons for its Purpose. Some knew what was afoot and were willing to serve, and in the front rank of these was Ibsen. He was a wholehearted believer in the poet as creator, not in any dependent or subordinate creating capacity, but as the very fount and origin of the beauty he brought into existence. It was life, of course, which worked within him, but life was something incapable of any rational explanation whatever. To Ibsen and Shaw it was a blind force dependent upon artists of honour for intelligible outlet and advance. A poet lent himself to life, and life did the rest. Ibsen used to be able to feel a play growing inside him like an embryo till in the end it quickened, kicked and burst out. He had one about every two years.

The first of them to come to London was *A Doll's House*. It was presented in 1889, and then came the Ibsen-row. There had just been a Wagner-row, but that had been a very select affair for musical critics. This new one was anybody's fight. The man in the street doesn't easily get worked up about music, but he gets wildly excited over discussions about the domestic affairs which Ibsen was using as material for his plays. He dramatised everyday situations with wonderful skill and insight, and yet allowed his characters to behave shockingly with a word of reproof. Women were unwomanly, and got away with it, and men were heroic and did not get away with it. There was the dickens of a row with people taking sides, writing letters, and calling names all over the place. There were disputes about stagecraft, children, religion, duty—about anything rather than the philosophy behind the plays. That, however, was what took Shaw's fancy from the beginning, and his *Quintessence of Ibsenism* was the result. Wagner had broken new ground, and conquered in music, and now Ibsen was coming with a new and wonderful message in drama. The world was changing, man was becoming conscious of his destiny, old institutions were crumbling, the dawn of the twentieth century was at hand, outworn moralities and cramping creeds must go, and all the rest of it. Shaw didn't lose his head about progress so badly as some of the others who wrote like this, but he believed in the message. He saw the theatre as the church of the new century and threw himself into the campaign for the New Drama and the New Morality with the same terrific energy and concentration that he had already shown in the cause of Socialism.

The *Quintessence of Ibsenism* is the keel of his dramatic career. In it he laid down the thesis and argument for all that followed, as firmly and definitely as he knew how. The argument was developed as a side issue in *A Perfect Wagnerite* (1898), thrown into dramatic form in *Man and Superman* (1902) and followed up with i's dotted and t's crossed in *Back to Methuselah* (1921). Whatever Shaw is, he is not erratic. He is the most carefully conscientious and consistent artist that ever lived. He may contradict himself, but he never wavers. In fact, from 1890, his philosophic career is dreadfully dull, so finally did he settle everything then and so exactly did he follow the regulations he prescribed. It is true that these are mighty queer and that his opinions and actions will look in turn blatant, nonsensical, extravagant, blasphemous, quixotic, and every other adjective of the kind, to anyone who tries to measure him by normally accepted standards—either those of the Christian or those of the commercial world. He lives in a world of his own, and his behaviour in it is correct to a degree which may well send cold shivers down the back of any happy-go-lucky sinner who dares turn a purely intellectual search-light on his own daily conduct.

The Ibsen ruction, Creative Evolution, the New Protestantism and the uprise of the artist prophets, all began with a fresh attempt to get a good answer to the question " What's a baby ? " The Middle Ages had it that he was something wonderful. Then came the Reformers, saying that Natural Instincts were Filthy and Babies a Bad Lot. This was too horrible for the average man, and the religious

history of Europe for the next four centuries is the
story of the ways in which he tried to solve the
question without going back to 1274. It did not
bother him so much while he was poor, but when the
Industrial Revolution made him rich and respectable
and he had more scope for sinfulness, his private
life became full of problems about women and
children. Ibsen took some of the strange situations
which he saw about him and touched them up with
a poetic hand into problem plays. Situations, real
and terrible enough in life, were turned into cases,
the new dramatic and literary art was launched, and
a new answer given to the question about the baby.

The poets were out to rescue him from the
agnostics and the super-Darwinists. The former
were getting a reputation for wisdom by saying that
they knew nothing, and that a baby was an
Unfathomable Mystery ; the others said that a baby
was built like a machine and that, given a free hand
with lancets and chloroform in an orphanage, they
could find out what made it tick. However crazy
the Creative Evolutionists look to-day, it must
always be remembered that they were at first a
rescue party out to save the children from the
ultra-rationalists. They had learnt—God knows
how—that a baby was something fresh and delightful,
and they wanted to protect him and give him a
chance to realise himself. They relied upon Evolution and they thought that any new child might be
the bearer of a message which would carry man a

further stage upward towards the Ultimate Purpose. His impulses must not be cramped by the credulities and customs of a bygone age—particularly of the age of reason. Old habits and old institutions were useful for children who had not the vitality to make their instincts imperious, but the exceptional infant must not be shackled by them. *His* impulses—*his* will to live—were all-important, and his impulse toward greater freedom was sufficient ground for the repudiation of any duty however sacred which conflicted with it. This was the New Protestantism in a nutshell.

Men like Ibsen and Shaw did not find the new religion as simple and delightful as it looked to their youthful disciples. For the child as he grew up had not only an impulse to realise himself, but another impulse to make the realisation reasonable. The exposure of ways in which he fooled himself in efforts to reconcile the two forces with one another and with existing conventions was the main-spring of the new drama. Some men were terribly reasonable and produced rigid irrevocable plays, others were full of imagination and wilfulness and produced irresponsible, wandering plays. In Brand and Peer Gynt the men were on a grand scale ; they were heroes all-of-a-piece, who clung to their ideals to the end. Later, Ibsen made plays with small-scale people fooling themselves in conventional ways, and arranged his action to show the gradual breaking down of the ideals which had upheld them. The discovery that plays could be made by this unmasking process had an effect on Shaw similar to his earlier discovery that fortunes could be made by rent collection. Henry George taught him that he had been a communist all along, and now Ibsen showed him that he had been a modern dramatist from the day of his letter to *Public Opinion*. *Immaturity*, *The Irrational Knot*, and the rest, were really plays which had taken the wrong turning. Their author was, in fact, the world's champion unmasker, but it had never occurred to him to make dramatic capital out of his talent.

He had made an attempt to collaborate with William Archer in writing a play in 1885 ; Archer was to supply the plot and Shaw the dialogue, but the Shaw dialogue ate up all the Archer plot in the first act, and the partnership was dissolved. Seven years later, stimulated by Ibsen, he completed *Widowers' Houses*, which, like an ugly duckling, pushed itself in amongst *The Private Secretary*, *Haddon Hall*, *The Guardsman*, *The Silent Battle*, *Dorothy*, and the rest of the legitimate brood on December 9th, 1892.

CHAPTER VI

In a fairy-tale world the ugly duckling gets a bad time because it is different. In the newspaper world conditions are reversed, and the thing that's different gets the magazine page. A motor-car manufacturer doesn't mind the public telling funny stories about his product if he knows the car will go. In fact, the wilder the stories are the better he likes them—publicity value being directly proportional to wildness. Shaw knew, as he watched that first performance of *Widowers' Houses* in December, 1892, that he could make plays that would go. The critics didn't think he could, nor did the public, and they continued to say so violently for days, to his great delight. It didn't cost him a penny, and everyone was being taught to say Shaw's a Socialist and Shaw's a Showman, and to look forward pleasantly to some sort of fireworks every time the name was mentioned.

Widowers' Houses irritated the public thoroughly. It pretended to be a play when it was really a dose of medicine. It contrasted violently with the standard play devised to amuse the audience, massage their emotions slightly, and send them home sleepy and comforted. The popular play of 1890 was, in fact,

very much like the popular film of to-day ; it was con-
structed so that it could be understood without any
mental exertion. The theatre was a place where
people were entertained by being soothed. Shaw
proposed to entertain them by making them think.
He had been doing a lot of thinking since 1866 and
he wanted to give everyone the benefit of it. Since
1882 the thinking had been running in a deep
economic groove, and when he tried to materialise
it dramatically, the effects were shocking. The
audience came to see a play and got the gist of the
Fabian Essay on Rent, wrapped up in the chatter
of nice people staying at the best hotels. There was
nothing gloomy about the scenes : all had their
share of bright lights, luxury and pretty dresses, and
there was nothing false about the story : blue books
were brought on the stage to certify the facts—but
the play was horribly unsettling. Many a decent
man with a few snug investments went to it, and was
bothered for days afterwards trying to find out where
Shaw was wrong. It was not so easy.

It took him a few years to find out that play-
writing of that sort was useless if he wanted to be
an artist with a public. And he wanted that just
as much as he wanted to set the world right. In
fact, the two wants are from the Creative Evolution
point of view indistinguishable, being in essence
nothing but the result of a sudden effort of the Life
Force at Synge Street, Dublin, in 1856. But this
merging and new mysticism is confusing to non-

initiates, and for the moment it is better to consider him as a very keen young man anxious to have his plays produced, and showing great practical intelligence in the way he went about it. He had always liked the theatre, and when he found that he could write plays that were playable, he began to study it with the greatest care from the playwright's point of view. After *The Philanderer* and *Mrs. Warren's Profession*, he knew that he could not get far by holding the microscope up to Nature, making people uncomfortable, and giving actors and actresses more than they could do. There were only a certain number of actors in London and a certain number of ways in which each of them could act. If Shaw wanted them to dance to his piping, he must make music to which they could dance. The plays of the 1894–1900 period are the result.

His adaptability was amazing. He wrote plays to suit a public, to suit a theatre, to suit one actor, to suit a pair of actors, but above all, to suit himself. From the very beginning he knew what he was after, and it did not turn him from his purposes in the least to have to turn out gay nonsense like *You Never Can Tell*, or sob-stuff like *Candida*. Beneath these cloaks George Shaw moved steadily and patiently about his business. He was a Fabian and knew that gradual action could be as effective in the theatre as in the committee-room—remember that he was busy with *Cæsar and Cleopatra* as he went to and fro, attending to the parochial affairs of St.

Pancras in 1898. He couldn't spring his ideas too suddenly on the public. He set them out boldly for the elect in his prefaces, but it was necessary to wean the people slowly and patiently. Infiltration was the best policy, and in *Candida* (1894), *The Devil's Disciple* (1897) and *Man and Superman* (1903)— or for that matter in any succession of his plays during the pre-war period—it can be seen at work. It can be seen even more clearly in his Dramatic Criticism in the *Saturday Review* from 1895 to 1898 when he worked week by week trying to get the public to bring their minds to the theatre with them, the actors to take some interest in the parts they were playing and people generally to see life as he saw it. In 1892 a dignified imperialistic newspaper tried to squash him with : " Mr. Shaw wishes to utter a tirade against certain abuses ; he thinks the theatre is a suitable pulpit for his utterances." That was exactly what he did wish and think, and he didn't mind who knew it. As he said himself a few years later :

> I am not an ordinary playwright. I am a specialist in immoral and heretical plays. My reputation has been gained by my persistent struggle to force the public to reconsider its morals. In particular, I regard much current morality as to economic and sexual relations as disastrously wrong ; and I regard certain doctrines of the Christian religion as understood in England to-day with abhorrence. I

write plays with the deliberate object of convert-
ing the nation to my opinion on these matters.
I have no other effectual incentive to write
plays, as I am not dependent on the theatre for
my livelihood. If I were prevented from
producing immoral and heretical plays I should
cease to write for the theatre, and propagate
my views from the platform and through books.
(*Prefaces*, p. 408.)

In the 'nineties he was dividing his time equally
between the political and dramatic roles, and his
purpose had not quite crystallised out in this clear-
cut, implacable form. He expressed it from time
to time in various ways, but his statements were
received with nods and becks and wreathed smiles
by a delighted public, who insisted on believing that
this living lump of dynamite was a droll fellow, who
was cashing in on his quality as a jester in a normal
business-like way. Many a prophet would have
despaired at such a slight. Instead, Shaw turned it
into an asset; he took the popular belief that he was
a clown, as a magic cloak, under which he had a
special licence to go anywhere and say anything.
Any intelligent government would have had him
and his like locked up; but it was the day of art for
art's sake, and Cabinet Ministers would have laughed
at the suggestion that plays had anything to do with
social upheavals.

He was wonderful. However disreputable his
doctrine, it is impossible to watch his work in these

years without wanting to get up and cheer—or is it only the untutored Irishman who wants to shout " Up, Man, though you burst the British Empire," at the sight of him backing his conscience against the world of rent and big business ?

He was far too wise to go out trying to start an open conspiracy. He was a soloist and he knew it ; and he was also a good deal of a child full of his own importance, going about—like Stevenson's boy with the dark lantern under his coat—full of tremors and anticipations. If you don't see him and love him like this you will never know him or understand his plays. It seems fantastic to say that an intensely serious social worker and a child playing at nursery tricks was one man, but he himself—or any reputable scientist—will tell you that the closer you get to facts the more fantastic they appear. Take these extracts from his letter to Ellen Terry (January 27th, 1897) :

> In this world, you must know all points of view, and take one and stick to it. In taking your side, don't trouble about its being the right side—north is no righter or wronger than south —but be sure that it is really yours, and then back it for all you are worth. And never stagnate. Life is a constant becoming, all stages leading to the beginning of others. . . . The theatre is my battering ram as much as the platform or the press . . . my capers are part of a bigger design than you think. Shakespeare

is to me, one of the towers of the Bastille and down he must come. . . . Never mind your young families ; omelettes were not made without breaking eggs, and I hate families. . . . What I say to-day everybody will say to-morrow.

There is the boy with his finger on his lips, his cloak and his conspiratorial air, full of cryptic sayings and dark hints of inside knowledge, playing at revolution and conquest with the most deadly earnestness.

There is no real right side. That is the essence of his faith and his preaching. In the Life Force there is no stable truth. To man in his little day there seems a passing permanence, a transient stability, a flattening out, on which Life seems to pause in its course, and which he calls truth. To linger on one of these facets, to cling to it, is to become imbedded in the past and to petrify. Life moves ever onward, and to move with it is to live . . . " kindness and truth and justice are not duties founded on abstract principles external to man, but human passions which have in their time conflicted with higher passions as well as with lower ones." . . . " Try how wicked you can be ; it is precisely the same experiment as trying how good you can be." . . . " There is no law so independent of circumstances that the time never comes for breaking it." So in *The Sanity of Art* (republished in book form ten years later), he continues to offer unweary-

ing witness to the intuitions which well up within
him.

. . . . .

Here is the New Protestantism at greater length :
The Life Force is blind. It shoots out in all
directions, but has a preference for none. It forms
instruments but has no plan for them. Man is
aware of its surging energy through his instincts,
and through the most powerful of them is made to
maintain the chain of vital energy with an annual
quota of young life. Each of these little ones comes
bearing with him millions of memories and messages
from the past, but also some potentiality of his own,
which is a special and sacred gift from the Life
Force. He feels this gift as his very self. It is his
inner citadel. He will stake everything to preserve
it. Beside it, even his own life is nothing. He will
not hand it over to any mortal man or to any earthly
power.

The Protestant enshrines the gift in a private
tabernacle ; he abhors Rome and the confessional,
because of his conviction that they threaten it. But
Shaw could see that an organised Protestant religion
was a contradiction in terms—an inconsequent copy
of the Catholic Church—and he concluded that the
religion of the twentieth century—the religion of the
Modern Spirit—must rest on some less institutional
recognition of that tabernacle. The New Protestantism must be founded on inward adoration of
one's own private judgment and outward toleration

of all men. Thus would the Life Force be given full scope ; thus would the artist be stimulated to his highest pitch of activity and at the same time freed from external restraints to self-expression. But there was one danger, there was one deadly enemy of the Life Force ; there was one intolerable person—the man who said that there were laws prescribed for men. The man who said that there were in the world rules valid at all times and in all places, must be eliminated ; he was the enemy of evolutionary advancement, and the institutions which he created on the basis of these rules were prisons for the children of the future.

An institution may be good for a time, for one year or a thousand years, but life moves on, and sooner or later some child is born with a potentiality which conflicts with the rules. The Life Force has no design, but is always trying, and each child is an experiment. He (or she, for the Life Force has no sex partialities) arrives ready stamped by some instantaneous impulse of the Time Spirit. The child who is to carry the torch of life onward and upward arrives earmarked for some special activity. He is predestinate. He must conform. To fulfil his destiny to perfection he must " find the point of view which is really his, and then back it for all he is worth." He seems to himself to have freedom, but this is an illusion ; he is not really free till he is doing the work for which he has been stamped out. He must stick to his cell. He cannot find his point of view by any rule or law outside of his own nature or by any established convention or by any imitation of others. There is no help to be had from outside. He can only find it by trial and error. His inmost wish is his guide, and that course of action which he can follow without qualms or doubts, and above all without shame or excuses, is for him the true way. It may be what others call murder, or cruelty, or adultery, or theft, or blasphemy, but these names must not deter if the sacred mentor within tells him to march fearlessly ahead. If the Life Force has not modelled him for a thief, then he will be downhearted in his thieving. If he is not meant to be a Don Juan, he will be uneasy in the love-nest. The experiment of being as wicked as he can must be abandoned, if it is not honestly successful. And it is just the same with experiments in being good. The boy who sets out to be a model to the community, and finds his pious practices a sham, and his week-day work a slavery, is being warned by the Life Force that he is in the wrong shop. The man who goes regularly to the Rotary Club, notwithstanding the spiritual nausea which rises up within him at the luncheon table, is ignoring sacred promptings. The wild impulse that comes over him at times to roar " To hell with Service," may be an inspiration direct from the Life Force. He cannot tell till he responds to it, till he *tries*. The trial may ruin him socially and financially, but if it brings him a sense of release—of refreshment

—of new life—then he knows that, come weal, come woe, he has committed a noble blasphemy.

Thus the Life Force taps out potentiality inspiration and at random . . . tinker—tailor—soldier—sailor—rich man—poor man—beggarman—thief . . . it pays no attention to parents or environment. The " rich man " urge may tap an attic in the slums, and the " poor man " urge a palace nursery. Then, if the urges are strong, that is, if the children " have the vitality to make their instincts imperious," the slum child rises to the palace and the other shakes the gold dust from his feet and goes out into the wilderness alone. It is the same with the soldier and the thief. A boy is born in Corsica with a love for power, and forty years later Napoleon is dominating Europe. Another boy is born in New York keen on easy money, and forty years later there is a rumpus on Wall Street and a new pleasure yacht sailing down the Hudson. These are the boys that matter. The rest, the weaklings, with their half-hearted wishes and feeble struggling activities, are Life Force failures, so much waste product, so much material for the master minds to turn into factory workers, clerks, journalists, economic experts, political props or anything else that may be required for the purpose in hand. They are, above all, copyists and imitators, and they love to be led.

This great group live on the rules laid down in the past, and on the standard conventions of the day. From them they make up the mental pictures which they call their worlds. When circumstances collect a large number of them with similar pictures into one place, it is called a suburb or perhaps a very exclusive club. But these waste products—these slaves—are not all alike. The first and commonest type is the hard-headed Philistine who gets through life pleasantly enough, because his nature and experience so closely match the picture he has selected, that he is barely conscious of his own existence. The second is the one hundred per cent idealist, who skips lightly over awkward facts, or, without qualms, twists them to fit his picture ; he has just as good a time as the first, in fact better, because his struggle with the facts make him proudly conscious of his picture and his relation to it ; he is righteous and he knows it. The third is the unfortunate who is partly conscious that his picture does not match reality, and his life is misery, or rather, he goes up and down in a sea of uncertainty, hysterically glad when facts fit, and distraught when they don't. Sometimes one of these unhappy ones sees, in a flash of inspiration, that part of his picture is wrong and that it is better to alter it than to fiddle with the facts ; sometimes even, the flash is so brilliant that it shows up the entire picture, releases him from the slave group and sets him free to move among the gods.

The gods are of two kinds. The first—the Class I god—is he who delivers the vital message unsullied, *i.e.*, untouched by the intellect. He is not troubled about rational behaviour, but works from day to day in perfect intimacy with the Life Force, relying on instinct and intuition. He is always ready with reasons if questioned, but makes them up to suit the occasion, and the querist. He goes after what he wants with absolute conviction and decides afterwards, if at all, why he wanted it. The Class II god is he who looks the facts of life fixedly in the face and sees that they sort out into a process of Creative Evolution. He is an ultra-rationalist, but his picture has none of the rigid fixity of the slave pictures. He knows that the reason for everything is that there is no reason for anything. His picture of reality is a moving picture to match the ever-changing world. It has neither form nor design—the deadly dogmatic prisons of the past—but shows in dim shimmering tones the Life Force striving to become conscious of itself. This is its great purpose—the purpose which holds together all pre-history, outline history and actual history. It is manifest through all human activity in man's pursuit of knowledge, particularly in those quests in which intuition outdistanced reason and gave birth to some great synthesis or enduring work of art.

Class II god is almost a new species. For him the difficulties of the past are wiped out. There are no problems of evil and pain, for it is clear that the Life Force working at random to fulfil its purpose must make mistakes, and that many things must go wrong before all comes right. There need be no anxiety about death and judgment, for there is but one world which is creating itself. Death, in fact, is only a rather interesting dodge by which the Life Force frees men from their self-importance when they have served its purpose. If they have served it well the manifold results of their good actions will be carried forward through the ages into everlasting communes. This is the meaning of life everlasting, this is the new revelation, so potent that since the beginning of the century new converts to Creative Evolution have been eagerly tearing away masks and showing their glowing, shimmering picture to all those fit to receive the message.

.   .   .   .   .

There were few fit for it in the 'nineties. In 1898 Shaw wrote in *The Perfect Wagnerite* :

> The majority of men at present in Europe have no business to be alive, and no serious progress will be made until we address ourselves earnestly and scientifically to the task of producing trustworthy human material for society. In short, it is necessary to breed a race of men in whom the life-giving impulses predominate before the New Protestantism becomes politically practicable.

That was the serious side of the business. But there was another side which must be viewed and considered although it is indescribable and presents an insoluble problem. Shaw's teaching and his plan of campaign are plain as a pikestaff, but there is an element running through it all which is a perpetual mystery. When he had laid down his creed and drawn the obvious conclusions from it in the most dogmatic and final fashion, the whole thing sometimes seemed to strike him as a tremendous joke. This was a point of view which his disciples were never able to understand. It annoyed them. Earnest Creative Evolutionists following him reverently and earnestly were suddenly brought up with a jolt against a peculiarly turned phrase which made them fear he had been pulling their legs all the time. He seemed to be able to have faith in his religion and at the same time view with amusement the possibility that it was all a hoax. He seemed at times to kick over the elaborate edifice he had so laboriously built—to throw science and scientists to the winds—to wrap a cloak of humility protectively about him, with a twist like—" Perhaps the world is all a joke—but even so, it is evidently our job to make it a good joke." He wound up a letter to Tolstoy with some words like those in 1910, but Russia and Ireland are far apart ; Tolstoy was busy making a religion of his own, with all laughs left out, and he only replied sadly : " I received a painful impression from the concluding words of your letter."

These sudden steps from certainty are disconcerting to his disciples ; but they are the very breath of life to the old-fashioned fellow, rather muddled at the mystery of the world in which he finds himself, and glad to get confirmation for his impression that it is all very puzzling and that the best he can do is to plug along hopefully in his own way, and give new gods a wide berth. When Shaw comes across any such man he seems to face right about from all his theories, and say : " It's rough going, old man, and we seem a bit off the track, but it's a great thing to feel we're all in the same blooming bus." This, at any rate, is the savour which rises from those touches of human sympathy that flash out in delicious asides through the action of his plays, particularly among the minor characters. He is at home with everyone, and even when he is going all out to mobilise humanity to march ahead with him under the banner of Creative Evolution, he is turning his head to shout after those going steadfastly in the opposite direction—Stick to it, boys, you're just as right as I am. There is no use making much of this anomaly, just yet, lest he retort, " But isn't this what I have been protesting against for fifty years? You are trying to work me out like an equation. I am not a sum. I'm alive."

All his dramatic work has to do with the slaves and gods and their pictures, but there is no prescription. There may be only one Class II god as in *Arms and the Man*, or one Class I god as in *St. Joan* or there may be one of each as in *Man and Superma* and *The Millionairess*. And even the gods are liable to show slavish traits at times, and the slaves to give a gleam of god-like quality. He makes a play by taking a group of ordinary individuals—Class I and Class II slaves—and turning them inside out. It is all done wittily, kindly, thoroughly, sometimes with the assistance of a Class II god and sometimes— but what's the use of trying to take that wonderful process apart when it is there to be revelled in at the source, for two shillings a copy. It is surprising value for money ; why, to watch him getting a play going and plunging his audience into the thick of the story before the curtain is up ten seconds is worth every penny of it.

He was studying the theatre and its possibilities as a revolutionary agency with the greatest interest, in the closing years of the century. For during those years his faith in the possibilities of social reform through political action was slowly dwindling. He was turning against Social Democracy as he found it in the flesh. He was testing his ideal of the 'eighties against the facts, and finding them wanting. The paragraph quoted above from *The Perfect Wagnerite* shows how his thoughts were tending, and they came to a focus in *Man and Superman* in 1902.

It was a wonderful play. It was three plays— it was a dozen plays—or maybe a hundred. It was a good straight comedy, it was a domestic drama, it was a sporting play about a motor-race, it was a mystery play, it was a play about a baby, it was a play for any audience. It is impossible to describe the effect of that startling, compact, subtle attack on basic convention and tradition; it is impossible in these hard-boiled, thick-skinned days to convey any impression of the tremors which ran through the theatre when the play was first presented in London (1905) and later in the provinces. The omission of the third act didn't matter, for its essentials saturated the others, and though no one could understand what Shaw was driving at, the sheer intensity of his thought made itself felt. Even if the meaning was hidden, it was evident he was saying something that was all the world to him, and saying it with remarkable emphasis.

He was. He was summing up the results of twenty years' experience as a reformer, confessing failure of the old method, and trying for a new one. He looked back and said that reforms were useless till man had reformed himself, and looked forward and said that man couldn't reform himself till the Life Force had reformed him. He cleared the decks of everything else in a single sweep—or rather in a series of them called a *Preface*, a *Philosophy*, and a *Revolutionist's Handbook*. He did it with that magnificent openness and thoroughness which is the joy and despair of his biographers—for it gives them the fullest inside information about him, and yet when they try to present it to the public, they find that it was all so much better in the original. So here are some extracts from *The Revolutionist's Handbook* to show the turning-point that had been reached :

A Revolutionist is one who desires to discard the existing social order and try another . . .

And yet

Revolutions have never lightened the burden of tyranny : they have only shifted it to another shoulder.

. . . . .

Are we then to repudiate Fabian methods and return to those of the barricader, or adopt those of the dynamitard and the assassin ? On the contrary, we are to recognise that both are fundamentally futile.

. . . . .

We must therefore frankly give up the notion that Man as he exists is capable of net progress. There will always be an illusion of progress, because wherever we are conscious of an evil we remedy it, and therefore always seem to ourselves to be progressing, forgetting that most of the evils we see are the effects, finally become acute, of long-unnoticed retrogressions ; that our compromising remedies seldom fully recover the lost ground ; above all, that on the lines along which we are degenerating, good has become evil in our eyes, and is being undone in the name of progress precisely as evil is undone and replaced by good in the lines along which we are evolving. This indeed is the Illusion of Illusions ; for it gives us infallible

and appalling assurance that if our political
ruin is to come, it will be effected by ardent
reformers and supported by enthusiastic patriots
as a series of necessary steps in our progress.

     •   •   •   •   •

Our only hope, then, is in evolution. We
must replace the man by the superman.

     •   •   •   •   •

The cry for the Superman did not begin
with Nietzsche, nor will it end with his vogue.
But it has always been silenced by the same
question : what kind of person is this Superman
to be ?

     •   •   •   •   •

What is really important in Man is the part
of him that we do not yet understand. Of
much of it we are not even conscious, just as
we are not normally conscious of keeping up
our circulation by our heart-pump, though if
we neglect it we die. We are therefore driven
to the conclusion that when we have carried
selection as far as we can by rejecting from the
list of eligible parents all persons who are
uninteresting, unpromising, or blemished without any set-off, we shall still have to trust to the
guidance of fancy (*alias* Voice of Nature), both
in the breeders and the parents, for that
superiority in the unconscious self which will
be the true characteristic of the Superman.

     •   •   •   •   •

As to the method, what can be said as yet except that where there is a will, there is a way? If there be no will, we are lost. That is a possibility for our crazy little empire, if not for the universe ; and as such possibilities are not to be entertained without despair, we must, whilst we survive, proceed on the assumption that we have still energy enough to not only will to live, but to will to live better.

·　·　·　·　·

There is no public enthusiast alive of twenty years' practical democratic experience who believes in the political adequacy of the electorate or of the bodies it elects. The overthrow of the aristocrat has created the necessity for the Superman.

·　·　·　·　·

The Revolutionist's Handbook is full of meat for to-day's eating. The *Quintessence of Ibsenism* had anticipated the new psychology with its introverts and inhibitions ; and Shaw had followed it up by showing that excellent psychological research could be done in parks and restaurants or any place where there were men and women not too much on guard ; the results were so interesting, and had such general application, that when he put them into plays they went down as well in Japan as in London. Now, on the basis of small-scale experiments in social and political work, he was reaching even more tremendous conclusions. Nearly thirty years before

Mussolini had noticed the "putrescent corpse of Liberty," it was being neatly laid out on a slab in the *Handbook*. Three years before the first paper on Relativity was read, Shaw had nailed up his thesis that man was a relative animal. Only the other day Sir James Jeans wrote : " It was left for twentieth-century physicists under the lead of Einstein, Bohr and Heisenberg to discover how large a subjective tinge entered into the nineteenth-century description of nature." Tinge ! Shaw entered the twentieth century shouting at the top of his voice that man was sunk to the eyebrows in subjectivity. He said bluntly that man always thought he was moving forward, but was in truth incapable of knowing whether he was or not. He actually called for a conference of enlightened persons to discuss what was to be done about breeding a superior type of man as the only way out of the tail-chasing mess ; at least Jack Tanner did so in his *Revolutionist's Handbook*. And then there was that incomparable first act, with Roebuck Ramsden, the modern thinker, backed by the bust of Spencer and the enlarged photograph of Huxley, saying : " Let me tell you I was an advanced man before you were born," and Tanner's mischievous, maddening retort : " I knew it was a long time ago." How the audience roared with delight at that conflict of dignity and impudence—without a notion that it was watching the first onslaught of the twentieth century on the nineteenth, of the relativists on the determinists.

And how they enjoyed its development a few seconds later :

> TANNER : . . . Cultivate a little impudence, Ramsden, and you will become quite a remarkable man.

> RAMSDEN : I have no——

> TANNER : You have no desire for that sort of notoriety. Bless you, I knew that answer would come out as well as I know that a box of matches will come out of an automatic machine when I put a penny in the slot. . . .

It was scandalously unfair, of course, to bring the poor old rationalist on the stage with his hands tied behind his back, and let the Life Force hit him in the face ; still that is what happens when a dramatist *grows* plays, instead of writing them to fit a framework. But no other plays grow like these, in which the Life Force slap-stick plays round at such a rate that it lays out even the Life Force prophet. There is no more deadly punch in this play than its final word :

> ANN (*looking at him with fond pride and caressing his arm*) : Never mind her, dear. Go on talking.

> TANNER : Talking !

> (*Universal laughter.*)

And the final curtain comes down on an audience once again a little bewildered and dizzy. "What does he mean ? ' Talking '—Is he making fun of us after all ? "

They could not be certain. And still less could

they see that his whole point was that there was no
certainty. There was a possibility that Man was
lost, but that was not a thing to be told to a crowd
of people, out for an evening's entertainment. It
was enough to give them a hint and cover it up in
" Universal laughter," but the facts were faced
frankly enough in the *Handbook*.

Society was failing to make itself. Man was not
yet up to the mark. Democracy in practice was a
failure. The New Protestantism would not become
politically practicable till the Life Force had shot
forth a new race of men. Meanwhile, the pioneers
must labour as inspiration dictated. Inspiration
came from the instincts—the impulses—the will.
Reliance on reason had been fatal, and rationalism
was slowly freezing over the natural outlets of the
human spirit. The will must come first. Jack
Tanner puts it neatly in his *Handbook*, " The man
who listens to Reason is lost. Reason enslaves all
whose minds are not strong enough to master her,"
as who should say, " Vernuft ist der Teufel's höchste
Hure."

The New Protestantism rests on the divine right
of private intuition. Reason, which at once rises in
revolt against a religion which would make her
play second fiddle, must be kept sternly in check.
She has her uses in the practical domain, but the
new prophets will not allow her to approach the
inner sanctum where Truth lies in the arms of the
Life Force.

159

Shaw quite openly looked on himself as a New Prophet. It was clear to him that it was so, and there was no need to be coy about it. The terrific self-assertiveness which sprang from this presumption kept him in constant hot water, but he didn't mind—not even when it chilled and he was told in icy tones that his behaviour was " bad form." It must be remembered that this was in the Edwardian period. Difficulties about Africa had been settled to the satisfaction of the statesmen of Europe ; the Empire was bigger and better than ever ; sofas were going out, and Chesterfields were coming in ; silks were getting softer and carpets thicker ; the Forsytes had weathered the storms of the 'eighties, and all round capital appreciation was in sight. Only those who belong to the bicycle age can understand what the phrase " bad form " meant in that England. It was the whole ten commandments in two words, and Shaw's " What is bad form to-day will be good form to-morrow" was as blasphemous as it was incomprehensible. He was beginning to practise his religion in real earnest by giving the most vehement and most public utterance he could of the truth that was in him.

Yet never was there a more considerate prophet. He almost effaces himself to give other prophets a chance. There is no paradox here, but only that strict logic which he always uses in practical matters. His religion demands that he must not only put forward his views with the utmost vigour, but

also that he encourage others to do likewise.
Emphatic statement is essential, but tolerance
must march along with it or even ahead of it.
All opinions, all art, all activities, so long as they
are honest, are equally valuable, till time sorts
out one from the others to build on it. So, a Life
Force prophet must beware of belittlement. There
is always the possibility that he may be a mistake,
and the other fellow the truth bearer. This is a
hard saying, but it is one that Shaw lives up to with
the most bewildering humility : it is impossible to
find clear proof of this in his own works, but all
young writers who have met him bear witness to it.
He seems to go out of his way to help those who
differ from him, though not without an occasional
mischievous twitch or two to test how firmly they
sit on the saddle. He wants artists to have absolute
freedom of expression even when he is wild with
them. In 1892, seeing Ellen Terry engaged in some
trivial part, he wrote :

> " I was furious. If I had been a god and had
> created her powers for her, I should have
> interrupted the performance with thunder, and
> asked in a fearful voice why she was wasting the
> sacred fire of which I had made her the trustee.
> But I knew she had made her powers herself
> and could be called to account by nobody for
> the use she made of them."

He went ahead with great gusto after he had nailed
his colours to the mast in 1903. He claimed freedom

for himself and for everyone else, and then set out to precipitate discussion on the proper regulation of this freedom in the best interests of the Life Force. What he really wanted was a nicely regulated Anarchism called Communism, but there is no use taunting him with this. He is well aware that his real problem is to know how much nonsense to stand from a superman before rounding on him.

He not only worked for the Life Force, but worked with it ; or rather it worked with him. He doesn't write plays—he grows them—he lives in the mind and heart of each of his characters in turn, and while that character is speaking, he and Shaw are, in a way, one person. Other artists have done the same thing, but not so thoroughly ; there is usually a real man to be found behind the play figures. In Shaw's plays there is only the Life Force aiming at nothing in particular, and everything in general. Or rather aiming at having the new religion accepted and everything that stands in its way rejected. The teaching is always well wrapped up—actors and audience get what they like—there are plenty of laughs and interesting situations ; but these things are only secondary to the main purpose of getting people to revise their views about marriage, punishment, criticism, history, politics and religion ; Shaw wanted them to look at things in the Life Force way instead of in the Christian way ; for the progress of the reforms he desired was being barred in all directions, by convictions based on Christian dogma.

It is not suggested for a moment that Shaw altogether scorned Christianity. He pointed out that Christ was a Life Force failure, but he always esteemed certain aspects of Christian teaching and frequently spoke highly of its social value. His pages are sprinkled with acknowledgments like : " I see no way out of the world's misery but the way that would have been found by Christ's will, if he had undertaken the work of a modern practical statesman " (*Prefaces*, p. 525). What he objected to, was the way in which people held on to the beliefs of A.D. 190 in the year 1900. He found these beliefs embedded in the social body, hidden and tenacious as the steel mesh in a great arch ; he saw that they were the real obstacle to reforms which he considered essential ; and he made no bones about attacking them. From *Major Barbara* (1905) to *The Simpleton of the Unexpected Isles* (1935) he has waged a steady campaign against them, preaching his alternative creed of life for life's sake.

But no one took him seriously. The Great War came and went and he hardly even changed his stance. People scarcely noticed *Androcles and the Lion* or its Preface. The play was a great success, for everyone liked to see a lion chase an emperor all over the place ; but it was not so easy to see that the play was a serious attempt to show the Life Force in action. Later, when *Back to Methuselah* was produced and published with labelled diagrams of his creed in every scene and page, people only yawned.

Then came the palpitating Life Force thriller, *St. Joan.* In London this was supposed to be a Christian play, because of the title, but there is a lack of internal evidence. The Joan of the play is a little like Lavinia who wasn't much of a Christian either—Androcles was worth ten of her. Joan is nothing but the physical receptacle of the Life Force striving onward and upward. As a Christian she lets the play down completely. Why, at the crucial point of the final act—the tearing up of her recantation—she makes a farce of the whole magnificent trial scene by talking like a second-rate nature poet, "if only I could still hear the wind in the trees, the larks in the sunshine, the young lambs crying through the healthy forest, and the blessed, blessed church bells that send my angel voice floating to me on the wind." Why, the minute any Inquisitor, who knew his business, heard that line, he'd have boxed the little impostor's ears and told her to get home to blazes and stop wasting his time. It doesn't need the Epilogue to ruin the play as a Christian epic.

He explains it all in the Prologue. Joan is a temporary materialisation of the Life Force endowed with an excessive evolutionary appetite. She is morally indistinguishable from the competent richy-bichy Epifania—the Millionairess. Each of them "has the vitality to make her instincts imperious." Each of them is an irrational appetite going after what it wants. Joan's actions look "higher," but in a Life Force world that is only a relative impression. In fact, Epifania, with her business sense, her energy and her talent for cutting out superfluous parts in the process of production, may yet come to be honoured as a superior type of female. Already the Joans who believe in God are being liquidated, and the Epifanias who believe in Efficiency promoted to executive positions in the new anti-Christian states.

This, of course, is horrible. But there is no use in running away from facts when they are unpleasant, or from hard thinking when it leads to curious conclusions. When a man starts with an impersonal Force enmeshed in matter, he winds up—if he is honest—with a pulpy world churned up by puppets who know neither good nor evil, nor anything but their own darkened wills.

No more need be said here of the playwright and the New Protestantism. It has now plenty of devotees and Shaw touches truth when he calls himself " the iconographer of the religion of my time." He has been its champion, but no one sees better its fatal weakness—its insoluble problem. He tries unceasingly for a solution. He tried in the *Preface on Bosses* (1935) but he got no further than in the *Preface to the Sanity of Art* (1907) when he wrote :

> I know no harder practical question than how much selfishness one ought to stand from a gifted person for the sake of his gifts, or on the

chance of his being right in the long run. The
Superman will certainly come like a thief in the
night, and be shot at accordingly ; but we
cannot leave our property wholly undefended
on that account. On the other hand, we cannot
ask the Superman simply to add a higher set of
virtues to current respectable morals ; for he is
undoubtedly going to empty a good deal of
respectable morality out like so much dirty
water, and replace it by new and strange
customs, shedding old obligations, and accepting
new and heavier ones. Every step of his
progress must horrify conventional people ; and
if it were possible for even the most superior
man to march ahead all the time, every pioneer
of the march towards the Superman would be
crucified.

You never can tell—with Supermen.

CHAPTER VII

SHAW is right. It is impossible in the dark cul-de-sac of Creative Evolution to know what to do about Supermen, Superwomen and Bosses generally. In that half-lit gloom, a man never can tell who's who, or even what's what. But why should he remain there? Why should he stay amid the topsy-turvy jigsaw if he claims to be a freethinker? Why should freethinkers cling to outworn dogmas which tie them down? Surely their datum should be Freedom, and not the dogma of the Propagation of Species wrapped up in some odds and ends stolen from the Christian wardrobe.

Who will write that great book—*Fun among the Freethinkers*? Professor Bury might have turned it out a few years ago, but he missed his chance. He took the freethinkers seriously, and wrote *A History of Free Thought*, 600 B.C.–A.D. 1912, instead. He set out valiantly to be the champion of thought, but that, as Shaw saw long ago, is a very slippery business. Many a man sets out bravely to blow thought's trumpet, and winds up sadly on his own horn ; but even that is better than falling in at the tail end of an Orange procession as Bury did. He meant well, but he only succeeded in showing how

elegantly a man of vast learning could say " To
hell with the Pope," and how evenly he could
match the steady thump of the Belfast drum as he
swung from " the lurid policy of coercion which the
Christian Church adopted " to " a velocity which
would have seemed diabolical to the slaves of the
medieval Church. He simply ate the spiritual food
which Gibbon offered in an uncritical mood.

The freethinkers have failed thought. They don't
think hard enough or freely enough, and they can't
keep straight. They go off on sidelines of their own,
scoffing at their pet antipathies or else trying to
make a new religion out of their pet fancies. Take
Herbert Spencer, one of the best of the old brigade.
He went his way trying to scatter the mists and get
down to something solid. He quarried back through
time and space in the regular way, till he could get
no further, and then said that beyond lay the
Unknowable. He decided reasonably enough that
there was no use trying to get any information about
a God that was unknowable, and then followed this
up, not so reasonably, with " therefore theology is a
self-destructive science." And *then* he began to set
out First Principles, showing conclusively that the
Unknowable was in general orderly and beneficent,
and in particular that It had the best interests of the
English upper middle classes at heart ; It disliked
militarism and doted on industrialism ; It was, in
fact, rather like Herbert Spencer.

All this went on chapter after chapter, and the cry

was taken up by Ramsden and the rest of them
without even a smile ; till Shaw came along in a gale
of laughter, and single-handed set out to free the
public mind from the bondage of Spencer and
Tyndall, and others less gifted, who were busily
scuttling the ship of thought under the impression
that they were sailing it towards the Great Awaken-
ing. But then, instead of being content with his
obvious job of mental masseur—instead of letting that
magnificent analytic gift rip into all the fakes of the
age to our dismay and delight—instead of sticking to
the things he could do so well—he took up theology
and went headlong down the same trap as Herbert
Spencer. With no capacity for abstract generalisa-
tion, with a knowledge of science only surpassed in
superficiality by his knowledge of Christianity, with
the eagerness and innocence of a child, he plunged
into a reformation campaign on behalf of a growing
synthetic God called the Life Force. It might just
as well be called Shaw. It is incalculable, it seeks
beauty and truth, it works by trial and error, it
makes mistakes and it is not in the least ashamed of
being inconsistent. In the exercise of these attributes it has produced an irrational universe which
it ignores in its preoccupation with a speck called
the earth where it fluked into self-consciousness
(*viâ* the giraffe), and where, after a series of unsuc-
cessful efforts at social organisation, it has been
greatly encouraged by the success of its most recent
experiment in Russia.

What chance has thought of freedom once it gets tangled up in this maze of home-made theology ? What is the use of throwing out water, however dirty, to drink from a spring befouled at its very source by a Power impersonal but purposeful ? And how can thought keep calm and collected when it looks facts starkly in the face, and finds that the said Power, with all eternity to experiment in, has only within human memory managed to replace buttons by zip fasteners ? Yet this Power—this Life Force— is the datum of the outstanding nineteenth-twentieth century freethinker. He claims that his creed is based on science, and has spent a lifetime trying to get people to found their institutions on " a genuinely scientific natural history " (*Prefaces*, p. 703). He wants sound ideas to " survive and be added to the body of ascertained knowledge we call Science " (*Prefaces*, p. 613). There is evidently a frightful mess somewhere. Free thinking, which should be a glorious, uncramped, out-thrust of the mind, has, for evolution worshippers, become a sort of mental debauchery on a Life Force treadmill. A modern freethinker is about as free as a freewheel, it moves about a fixed centre and turns only in one way— away from facts, away from common sense, away from reality.

There is one sound idea which has now survived for nearly a century and shows every sign of surviving for ever ; but those who adore the Life Force reject it. It was " added to the body of ascertained knowledge we call science " before Shaw was born, and has slowly but surely gained such a commanding position that all old laws acknowledge it or perish, and all new laws bow to it before admission. The ordinary man knows this law so well that he doesn't notice it. He relies on it to make things hot or keep them cool just as he relies on the law of gravitation to keep things in place when he uses a paperweight. Engineers find the idea infinitely reliable and call it the second law of thermodynamics, but this need not disturb the layman. He knows, just as well as any engineer, that the sitting-room fire will go out if he doesn't put on coal, and that his coffee gets cooler as he reads his morning paper ; even if he uses a thermos jug or a radium quilted cosy, he isn't fool enough to think that he can keep his coffee warm for ever. He may know that he could heat the coffee by stirring it, but, if he does, he also knows that he would be fighting a losing battle. The engineer says that the universe tends towards thermal equilibrium, or, if he wants to be frank, that material energy is fizzling out. We are living in a world where things get colder and colder. This straightforward summing up is as good a way as another of regarding the most reliable and inexorable of scientific laws ; it is the next thing to omnipotent ; it governs all actions connected with food, clothing and shelter ; every ship, every train, every motor-car, every aeroplane, depends upon it from minute to minute and day to day.

And it is perfectly dependable ; it seems a nuisance
to those who are trying to keep the soup warm,
but they must remember that they could never
have warmed the soup at all if the kitchen stove
had not been willing to get cooler, and let them
also remember that what they lose on the soup they
make up on the ices. Everyone believes in the
second law of thermodynamics whether he knows
it or not ; he is as sure of it as he is that the sun
will rise to-morrow morning, and continue to part
with some of its heat to keep him alive ; it is the
most certain of all the laws of science ; all phenomena move smoothly to its bidding, nowhere has a
single event been found to conflict with it, all
movement, all energy, all warmth, all physical life,
is in its keeping ; it has a right to rule the domain
of science which no sensible man can question.
To thrust it aside is to thrust science aside, but to
acknowledge it is to ruin evolution as a religion.
There is here an obvious dilemma, but it does not
seem to worry either the Communists or the
Racialists or even British biologists who face both
ways for the Advancement of Science. Neither
Russians nor Germans nor the others seem to be so
fully aware of the dilemma as Shaw, but he, as will
be seen in the next chapter, appears to be able to
face both ways with comparative comfort.

The evolution worshippers try to evade the law
by refusing to admit facts and be ruled by reason.
They argue that it is not right to apply universally

the conclusions reached from laboratory experiments or from observations limited to the surface of the earth. This would be fair enough if they stuck to their guns. But they daren't. They argue this in one breath and in the next they extol Galileo and Newton for jumping to conclusions about the universe from observations on a pendulum and a falling apple. And then after a few jibes at the ecclesiastics who tried to obscure the work of Galileo they come back and do their little best to obscure the splendid work of Kelvin. They object to the conclusion that the universe requires a real God to keep it going, because it is derived from manœuvres with a gas engine, a thermometer, a jug of water, a balance and some weights ; and yet at the same time they are working with a foot rule, a few fossils, some pigeons and a dozen sliced guinea pigs to demonstrate the existence of an eternal evolutionary God enmeshed in matter and for ever at the mercy of its unintelligence. They miss the ever-growing glory of Kelvin's synthesis as it spreads out from the laboratory, calmly taking all natural facts in its stride, and smoothly ordering every phenomena it meets. And they patch and twist Darwin's theory into an unrecognisable complexity as they feverishly try to make it fit the new knowledge which daily threatens to wreck the version they repaired only yesterday. They want things both ways, but they must eventually face facts and common sense, which unite to say that things are cooling down, that the material world is dying ; that, if this law be not accepted as universally applicable, science has no authority even in its chosen sphere, and there is no ascertained knowledge, no evolution, no truth, no beauty, nothing but Man—as Ampère said— drowning helplessly in his own spit. On the other hand, if the law be accepted it is possible to find room for freedom, love, order and all other things Man cares for, there is even room for evolutionary theories, but evolutionary dogmas, evolutionary religions, and the Life Force God must go.

All this was as well established in 1851 as it is to-day. But the scientific journalists, and even some of the scientists, were so busy with Lamarck, Darwin, Huxley and Haeckel, that they ignored the other great team—Carnot, Clausius, Joule and Kelvin. It was easier to learn to spell " protoplasm " and " metabolism," and later, even " masochism," than to grasp the principles of physics. In 1887 Kelvin wrote : " I had the great pleasure for many years, beginning just forty years ago, of making experiments along with Joule, which led to some important results in the theory of thermodynamics. This is indeed one of the most valuable recollections of my life, and is indeed as valuable a recollection as I can conceive in the possession of any man interested in science," but people carefully ignored science when it affirmed the necessity for a Creator as the new physical synthesis did. They could not get enough of it

a few years later, when the new biological synthesis
affirmed the opposite. Business was good, Manchester—Joule's town—was getting ahead, there
were fortunes to be made in ships and railways ;
to the twinkling amusement of the stars, and the
tumultuous laughter of the sun, men fell down in
adoration before the steam engine, and up rose a
mighty chorus :

> O Perfectly Reversible,
> We're very far from Thee.
> Lead on Thy slaves coercible
> To Great Efficiencee.

Gathered about rocks and fossils and the internal
organs of rabbits there were other groups of worshippers, rapidly growing unbalanced by the
wonders unfolded to them, and forgetting that if
science is not one, it is nothing. Word spread out,
not so much from them as from their literary hangers-
on, that Nature made itself, that miracles couldn't
happen, and that the world was getting better and
better. But there was no publicity at all for the
other scientists, who, sticking closely to facts and
straight thinking, were showing in the clearest
possible way that material things couldn't create
themselves, that Nature itself was a miracle, and
that the world was slowly and surely running down.

Science, smiling like the Cheshire cat, offered its
devotees two vehicles. One was marked " Going
Up "—a ramshackle conveyance with some essential
links missing. The other was solid as a rock and

had everything spick and span, but was marked
" Going Down." The joke was obvious enough ;
but it had also hidden depths, for all the tools needed
to start Bus No. 1 and keep it running were manufactured and stored on Bus No. 2.

There was a tremendous rush for the first Bus.
Social Democrats, Anarchists, Marxists, Psycho-
analysts, Uplifters, Lords and Ladies, Tired Business
Men, Novelists, Dramatists and Poets offering pæans
to the Life Force, all clambered aboard and started
off at full speed. At least, the wheels began to go
round at a great rate. Bus No. 2 was unpopular, for
apart from the disconcerting sign, it contained only
one non-upholstered compartment marked " For
Hard Thinkers Only." Still it was boarded by a few
audacious spirits—Michael Faraday dropped in for
a little while to say good-bye to Clerk Maxwell ;
Gregor Mendel worked away by himself in a quiet
corner. . . .

The first Bus rattled away like mad till somewhere
between the discovery of radium, in 1898, and the
Treaty of Versailles, in 1919, there were a series of
smashes, and the passengers were finally thrown out,
to find that the Bus hadn't budged an inch, and
that Science, gradually vanishing and smiling more
widely than ever, was offering them a new con-
traption like a merry-go-round. The signs Up and
Down were also vanishing, and a new sign—
Going as you Please—was coming into view. The
new roundabout was called Relativity, and there

were all sorts of seats in it, except Right seats. Passengers could think anything at all, provided they thought as they pleased, and didn't trouble too much about the real common-sense world.

Thought was too hard a mistress. That was the core of the trouble. Man deserted her and sought more pliant and accommodating partners. He lured the lissom Intuition from her natural home, and went dancing with her towards the mountain-top . . . and suddenly found himself alone with the wild-eyed infant, Contradiction, clinging to him like a young octopus. Science split first into two, and then into ten thousand parts. The intelligentsia switched from " Every man his own priest " to " Every man his own scientist," and Metaphysical Vitalism was born.

It works like this. The M.V. takes his stand on his favourite facts, and appeals for public support as a metabiological scientist and modern thinker. In due time an opponent collects enough conflicting facts to make mincemeat of the new thought, and just as he is doing this in a perfectly decent and rational way, he finds that the M.V. has bolted from reason and reality to his inner intuitional tabernacle, and is calling out in a voice charged with emotion : (1) that he is full of exultant resignation, or (2a) that he is proudly defiant of the trampling march of unconscious power, or (2b) Down with Aristotle, or (3) Do let us be nice to one another, or (4) Down through the ages intolerance

has ever dug the grave of truth, or (5) Wretch !
Viper ! ! Muck raker ! ! ! . . . There are as many
defences against facts as there are Metaphysical
Vitalists, but they are all alike in their flight from
reason, and their appeal to emotion. Shaw's
counter to Kelvin was a song and dance to the tune—
Away with Melancholy, trust the Life Force. (*Pen
Portraits and Reviews*, p. 165.)

The old science was founded on faith in the
uniformity of Nature, or in other words, the dogma
of the GOODNESS OF GOD. The new science of Bus
No. 1 started from the dogma of the Propagation of
Species. The trouble did not begin there either,
for the split in science was brewing from the time
when real faith began to evaporate, and Newton
began to turn Unitarian because he couldn't find an
equation for the Trinity. The drying-up process
was slow, and science was able to live on the savings
of the past while it advanced by leaps and bounds
towards the twentieth century. Then the really
mad part of the story started. Scientific laws had
been gradually removed from their natural foundation and based on the notion that all events were
entirely "caused" by other events. A Scotchman
had pointed out that this was nothing but a hunch,
and scientists, rather flummoxed and unwilling to
retrace their steps, had to dignify the hunch by
giving it names like "vital intuition" and "inex-
pugnable belief." Science, running away from
metaphysics, continued its headlong charge faster

and faster, but now a little bit like a horse on roller skates.

Not only were the laws lifted from their natural resting-place, but—here the story gets madder still—the book-bred brigade, that had learnt a few of the laws by heart, began to use them as pickaxes to remove the foundations altogether. They spread abroad the new faith that a real Creator was unnecessary, and that an imaginary Creator, trampling and blundering along, was the only God fit for the modern mind. The old idea of a God that saves men was discarded for the new one of men that save God. The inner circle began " disencumbering Christianity from the accretions which deform it," and "redistilling the eternal spirit of religion." Even genuine scientists became affected, and some are now to be found patting Nature reproachfully on the head and telling her that she is not very Efficient. For instance (see *Nature*, June 16th, 1934, p. 897) :

> The protection for the embryos is admirable, but almost over-ingenious since the object in view—the propagation of the species—is somewhat defeated when so many good seedlings must eventually perish.

This is science of the twentieth century ; the facts are admitted but they are " defeating the object in view." An old-fashioned scientist would have said, " We must alter our opinion about the object in view," and an ordinary man with normal common sense would say that Nature is on her knees to him, begging him, beseeching him, to notice that she is a prodigal mother; that she does everything on a lavish, magnificent scale; that she hates " efficiency"; that she throws the very energy of the sun wildly in all directions into space, so that the one tiny morsel on which man is born may be nourished and give forth wheat, coal, and everything he needs in reckless abundance. This view may be only a provisional hypothesis, but it fits the facts; it is the normal view which a man would take if he hadn't received a modern secular-sectarian education, and if he got a chance to look at the phenomena about him sensibly, but it is no longer scientific because everything must be trimmed to fit the dogma of the Propagation of Species. Common sense is no longer of any use. Nature is defeating the object she has in view! She is, in fact, " bad form," but now that this has been pointed out in a great scientific journal, Nature will presumably have to mend her ways and be governed as nearly as possible as we might suppose her to govern herself were she in her right mind.

It is not easy for an evolution-obsessed generation to see that Christianity is all of a piece, and that it is impossible to get ahead by taking over the parts of it that attract, combining them with the latest scientific news, and calling the result the religion of the twentieth century. Shaw can't see it even yet. He said in 1910 :

To me God does not yet exist ; but there is a creative force constantly struggling to evolve an executive organ of god-like knowledge and power. . . . To my mind unless we conceive God as engaged in a continual struggle to surpass himself—as striving at every birth to make a better man than before—we are conceiving nothing better than an omnipotent snob. (Letter to Count Tolstoy, quoted in Henderson's *Bernard Shaw*, p. 529.)

and he was still at it by proxy in 1932 :

" My own belief is that he is not all he sets up to be. He's not properly made and finished yet. There's somethin' in us that's dhrivin' at him, and somethin' out of us that's dhrivin' at him, that's certain ; and the only other thing that's certain is that the somethin' makes plenty of mistakes in thryin' to get there. . . ." Nothing would ever persuade him that God was anything more solid and satisfactory than an eternal, but as yet unfulfilled, purpose. (*Adventures of Black Girl*, p. 55.)

This may be very convincing to men over fifty, but children want to know why they should care about a Force which doesn't care about them, and why they should trust a God that is still experimenting with matter and still making mistakes— earthquakes, for instance—after having had all eternity to practise in. Why should a boy of spirit make himself the slave of a deity who may have a cosmic sneeze any day, and send the solar system to smithereens (see Chapter X, " Exploding Stars " in any modern Astronomy). The God of Creative Evolution can't stand on its own legs one minute before any sensible boy's curiosity. The God of Creative Evolution crumples up daily and Shaw has had to borrow from Christianity all along the line, the wherewithal to prop up his deity and make it presentable.

He launched the Life Force in the first place by taking the first and last articles of the Apostles' Creed and thinning them down into forms which couldn't possibly startle anyone. Then he brought old-fashioned words and phrases into the evolutionary swim with such word-play as—" Conscience is the most powerful of all the instincts, and the love of God is the most powerful of all the passions " (*The Christian Commonwealth*, July 20th, 1910). Later he dressed up his deity in scraps torn from St. Paul and St. Thomas Aquinas ; as in the Epilogue to *Back to Methuselah* when Lilith tells how Man and Woman :

> Press on to the goal of redemption from the flesh, to the vortex freed from matter, to the whirlpool in pure intelligence that, when the world began, was a whirlpool in pure force.

Only the year before last (1935) he borrowed the Day of Judgment ; but the most audacious borrowing of all was done when he kidnapped St. Joan to exploit her as a sample of supercharged Life Force groping its way towards " higher things " . . . and yet, in a sense, it may also be said that St. Joan borrowed Shaw to write a play in her honour and in justice to her age—but she let him write the Preface and the Epilogue himself !

Here again is that elusiveness, that duality, which evades analysis. He borrows, but he gives back . . . and then takes away again. He raises his hands in reverence, and puts his fingers to his nose in a single gesture. He bases his religion on science, and then makes his science a laughing-stock by grouping phenomena into " facts " and " mistakes." He travels with the crowd on Bus No. 1, and yet he is not of it. He is a freethinker, but he does not delude himself like the other passengers that he is ruled by reason. When he falls back on his emotional hunch and says, Trust the Life Force, he is not, like others, beating a retreat, but re-entrenching himself at his starting-point. He knows that the others are fooling themselves by finding reasons for what they have already decided to believe or disbelieve ; and his mischievous sallies on this point fill them with speechless indignation.

Shaw began by kicking reason out of the front door and then he rushed to the back door to let her in. He can't get on without her, but he likes to pretend he can by admitting her under new names, like " conscience " and " self-control." He wrestles mightily and unceasingly with her, moving so swiftly that no one has ever been able to label him "This side up." An unwary opponent once tried to get the better of him with "But, Mr. Shaw, you speak like two separate persons," and was dumbfounded by the reply, "Why only two?"

He has never abandoned the stand he took up in the *Quintessence of Ibsenism*, where he argued that "the will" has the first word and the last word, and that reason is only so much mechanism for subordinate uses. "Only the other day our highest boast was that we were reasonable human beings. To-day we laugh at that conceit and see ourselves as wilful creatures." That was when he was thirty-three. At thirty-nine he was still able to write, on p. 323 in *The Sanity of Art*, "life is the satisfaction of a passion in us of which we can give no rational account whatever," and "the setting up of reason above will is a damnable error," but this was after he had hobbled the will on p. 321 with: "The moral evolution of the social individual is from submission and obedience as economisers of effort and responsibility, and safeguards against panic and incontinence, to wilfulness and self-assertion made safe by reason and self-control," and "Without high gifts of reason and self-control, that is, without common sense, no man dares yet trust himself out of the school of authority." In 1921 after the Hang-the-Kaiser election and the Treaty of Versailles, he put on still heavier hobbles with :

THE GREATEST OF THESE IS SELF-CONTROL

As there is no place in Darwinism for free will, or any other sort of will, the Neo-Darwinists held that there is no such thing as self-control. Yet self-control is just the one quality of survival value which circumstantial selection must invariably and inevitably develop in the long run. . . . What *is* self-control? It is nothing but a highly developed vital sense, dominating and regulating the mere appetites. To overlook the very existence of this supreme sense ; to miss the obvious inference that it is the quality that distinguishes the fittest to survive ; to omit, in short, the highest moral claim of Evolutionary Selection : all this, which the Neo-Darwinians did in the name of Natural Selection, showed the most pitiable want of mastery of their own subject, the dullest lack of observation of the forces upon which Natural Selection works. (*Prefaces*, p. 504.)

The wrestling match never ceases. In the last passage, reason seems to be winning hands down, but one never can tell with Shaw. She may be winded any minute by a jab like " Conscience is the most powerful of all the instincts," or paralysed by a sudden twist like " We still have the silly habit of talking or thinking as if intellect were a mechanical process and not a passion." It is impossible to follow the ups and downs of this contest, for, as can be seen, and as will be shown more clearly in the next chapter, he makes his own meanings for words as he goes along. The " will " appears to be sometimes an undefinable mystery, sometimes one of the sensitive appetites, sometimes intuition, sometimes what people call the heart, but never the rational appetite. This being so, he is on firm ground when he says that the setting up of reason over " will " is a damnable error. It certainly is. It has been responsible for most of the heresies which have afflicted Christendom ; the rest being due to the diabolical error of setting up " will " over reason. Shaw is the only man of note who has ever been able to take a hand in both heresies simultaneously, or at least on alternate days, and it must make him feel like a lot of different persons—but two is enough. He is perfectly reasonable about everything but reason, and a great freethinker about everything but thought ; still, she will beat him in the end and grind to dust everything in him that does not pass fairly through her mill. Some minds may be temporarily paralysed by the strain of trying to assess all human faculties in terms of " survival value," but this fashion will pass. Or, if it does not, and if men will not be taught by common sense and reason that Bus No. 1 never brings its passengers anywhere, they will inevitably find themselves being taught by the brutal and primitive process of trial and error. 1914–1918 was only a trial in a tea-cup ; the next event, for which preparations are now being so feverishly made in Europe, will be an error on a new scale—a mighty smash if it comes off—but such smashes are all in the day's work for the Life Force.

For the Life Force Bus is still on the road. It has been amalgamated with the Merry-go-round, and become a Phantom Bus for Materialistic Mystics. Within it, survival-value is the only value, and trial-and-error the only test of truth. It is curious that Shaw should be so absolutely wrong and yet so relatively right ; it is as though he had been born aboard that Bus and, in his indomitable efforts to make it into a true home for men, had revealed its absurdity. What passengers it carries ! Some try to travel with it, keeping one foot on the running board and the other on solid ground ; some, in priestly robes, try to Christianise the Bus with one hand while they Modernise their churches with the other ; some try to grab the wheel and drive anywhere, just for the sake of driving ; some try, humourlessly, to drive onward and upward ; some try to collect the guns and keep order ; but the vast majority say " we've only one life to live " and make for the seats with the most luscious looking-upholstery. Shaw, the playwright, has had his eye on the whole unwicked-unholy cargo of them for fifty years, and has given us a wonderful picture of the antics of one elegant group as they flirt and fiddle in a cosy corner. It is called *Heartbreak House*.

It is curious, too, to see how some of his dreams have come true. The Supermen have arrived and every step of their progress is horrifying conventional people, respectable morality has been emptied out and replaced by new and strange customs, marriage has been modernised, kings have been kicked out, old obligations have been shed. It is, as Shaw said in 1897, impossible to make omelettes without breaking eggs, but since then eggs have been smashed by the million all over Europe and where are the omelettes ? In Russia ? In Germany ? Or perhaps in Spain ? It is easy to see the Life Force at work in its own peculiar way on these fronts, and there are plenty of crushed shells on its track, but what has it brought forth that a free man with hope in his heart cares to eat ?

It is worth considering some of these terrible attempts at omelette-making. It is difficult to get reliable information from Russia but it may be assumed that M. André Gide, who has been studying conditions there, would not be easily misled nor willing to make things appear worse than they are. It is well to remember here, that Shaw and Webb see in the Russian experiment the partial realisation of their dearest hopes of the 'eighties, and the practical demonstration of the value of their Life Force (or Social Organism) teaching. Webb has recently written a book to show how splendidly the Communist experiment is progressing, and Shaw puts on his most beautifully tinted spectacles when he writes of the wonderful work of the Soviets :
" Now Russia has shot ahead of all the Powers in

combining an intense public activity with an extension of popular initiative and individual freedom beyond the power of workers under Liberal Capitalism ever to conceive " (G.B.S. in *G. K.'s Weekly*, March 21st, 1935). M. Gide, summing up in 1937 what he actually observed in Russia, says that nowhere in the world is " the spirit less free, more humiliated, more terrorised, more enslaved."

Or take the facts and judge for yourself. Read the Preface to *The Simpleton of the Unexpected Isles* and see how a man who all his life has fought for humanity against cruelty and bestiality can allow the Life Force belief to steel his heart and cloud his mind, as he writes to defend Russian terrorism and excuse mass butcheries. And then read some reliable report of the recent execution of the group of outstanding army officers and try to assess the value of this latest outburst of egg-breaking. Is it a glorious demonstration of the advance of the human spirit or is it something fiendish? Is the Soviet chorus of demanding the death of the " poisonous pygmies " and calling for " a cur's death for curs " a dignified accompaniment to the administration of justice? Is the outpouring of the Bolshevist poet laureate Biedny : " We are ashamed of the mothers who bred such dirty dogs. These curs have poked their muzzles into the Fascist food trough "—and all the rest of it, likely to raise the standard of Russian literature ? These are points on which the normal man is just as

competent to give a useful opinion as any literary
genius. And, even on the " survival-value " theory,
it is the normal man who will in the long run decide
whether the omelettes are eatable.

The way of the Life Force in Germany is not so
very different. The rulers there use internment
camps instead of explosive bullets, but they are
equally insistent on replacing the Trinity by the
State, and, to that end, are waging a strong campaign to smash ancient beliefs and produce a
national sentiment which is simply the New Protestantism in a politically practicable form. In Russia
and Spain the Life Force works in a rough-and-
ready, slaughter-house way but in cultured Germany
it is necessary to garnish the omelettes a little, and,
when serving them, to use some of the religious
phraseology to which the people are accustomed.
Listen to Herr Hitler's speech of March, 1936 :

> My German compatriots, there is very
> much which we have to make good before our
> own history and before our Lord God. Once
> His grace was upon us ; and we were not
> worthy to keep it. Providence withdrew its
> protection from us, and our people were put
> down, put down deeper perhaps than any
> people before. In this dire need we learned to
> pray once more. We learned to respect one
> another : we believed again in the virtues of a
> people : we tried again to be better. So there
> arose a new community, and this people of

to-day can no more be compared with the people that lies behind us.

This is the usual attempt of the New Protestant to draw a cheque on the Christian account by presenting the credentials of " grace " and " prayer " and even a " Lord God." Behind it there is nothing but a pantheistic vagueness, a weird racial Power, the Life Force over again—this time wearing a German mask, and making ingratiating overtures to the Aryan race with promises of bigger and better omelettes. Let Russia or France or England or the prisoners in the internment camp stand in the way of this emerging God at their peril. It knows nothing but the German State and cares for nothing but its interests.

In England the line of division between the New Protestantism and the Old is becoming more and more blurred. The new religion is making headway in a peacefully penetrative way and so far there has been no open conflict between the omelette makers and the traditionalists who hold so tena‚ ciously to the old beliefs. But last year the world was started by a spectacular challenge from the Life Force to the most ancient of English institutions. It did not look like that, in fact it seemed to be quite a romance and not at all like a threat from the new culture to the old ; but the Life Force has many masks, and always accommodates itself to national sentiment ; in England it is known as the Modern Spirit.

This statement may seem strange. It may be argued that the Russian Life Force is savage and the German Life Force arrogant, and that neither has anything in common with this well-mannered Modern Spirit which moves so easily in the best circles and is so well dressed and respectable. Of course it is. Where could more highly respectable citizens be found than the Englishmen who launched the evolutionary doctrines which cut at the very root of the beliefs on which all lasting British institutions are based ? Or, if nineteenth-century writers are supposed to be out of date, take the views of a modern young Englishman who is neither savage nor arrogant. It is just a standard sample of what hundreds of other honest intelligent young Englishmen with literary gifts and no observable critical faculty, are repeating like children repeating a lesson : " In the last two centuries with ever increasing acceleration this natural rhythm, this static conception of life have been breaking down. . . . The old agricultural-religious basis is crumbling away, a totally new sort of life is coming into being through a profound revolution, in which the World War was no more than a bloody and reactionary episode. Most of our standards and beliefs and institutions seem obsolete." It is impossible not to sympathise with him as he tries to fight his way out of the mess into which three centuries of twisted thinking have landed him, but there is no use pretending that this sample of the Modern Spirit is anything but plain continental Life Force, or, if preferred, a redistillation of the Metaphysical Vitalism of *Back to Methuselah*. It is old-fashioned evolution dope not very different from that served out by Rosenberg and Hitler, as may be seen by comparing it with the quotations on pages 40 and 190. It is the old Life Force story over again, warmed up with the energy of youth and crisped into neat paragraphs in *John o' London's Weekly* (June 11th, 1937). The story is always the same—the old beliefs are no longer any use, the old law is no longer binding, the man of to-day is not as the man of yesterday, a new species is being created—and how can a young fellow resist when a spell-binding leader, or a wonderful Inner Voice, tells him that his children are going to be gods ? This is always the promise in that well-worn story, but it never comes off ; the children are always slaves ; and if those who still have faith in the old beliefs and the old law do not stand by them and fight for them, the new species of enslaved men will be created in England as surely as in Russia or in Germany.

They will not notice the process. It will be presented to them as a wider and larger life—" life " being pictured as some type of omelette attractive to the national palate. The Inner Light will be deflected and dimmed and brought down to shine on some scheme of social organisation, or production, or credit reform, or education, or armament, which, however stupid or unreal, can usually be made to look attractive for a time in that wonderful glow. " If our political ruin is to come it will be effected by ardent reformers and supported by enthusiastic patriots as a series of necessary steps in our progress." Isn't Shaw wonderful ? *The Revolutionist's Handbook* is even more up-to-date to-day than it was in 1902. The slaves don't know they are slaves ; in Russia the Sovieteers believe that they are escaping capitalistic exploitation, in Germany the Nazis walk with a firm step and their chins up. Do they feel cramped and confined ? Not a bit of it ; they smile at England's effete condition, and its fumbling efforts to keep the shabby idol of democracy in repair. And on the " concept of evolution onward and upward " are they not right ? By what authority does the Englishman, full of the Modern Spirit, discarding the rules *he* doesn't like, condemn the foreigner, full of the Life Force, for scrapping the rules which don't suit *him ?* On what basis do they settle any dispute which arises between them ? And what is to prevent the Life Force from tearing Europe to pieces to find out which of it is right ?

But perhaps this is going a little too far. The Englishman is a strange person. He is fond of fancy beliefs in theory, but in practice he likes to stand by the old formulæ which have stood so well by him. It makes him feel Modern to have some divorce laws on his statute book, just as it makes him feel broad-minded to have a few bawdy stories his repertoire. But when it comes to action it is different. He values the formulæ, even when he doesn't understand them, and he has little use for those who don't stand by them. Perhaps some day he will try to find out where the formulæ came from, and be surprised to learn that they are " rationalisations of experience firmly keyed to reality." And he will learn, too, that the Commonwealth based on big business and the big stick is a sham, and that the only enduring common wealth of man comes from common sense and common creed.

And when that day comes ; when the pioneers of knowledge regain their faith and their sense of reality, and Science is again one ; when all that remains of the glamorous religion of Creative Evolution is buried under the dull respectability of a solidly entrenched hypothesis ; and when the Life Force under a new name is playing hell with a new generation of intelligentsia ; some day, sooner or later, the clarity of vision which went to the making of those plays and prefaces will get its due, and they may yet stand as a permanent record of the period of the evolutionary nightmare, when so many lived in a world of muddled emotionalism labelled mysticism, and self-splurges labelled creative activity; a world of magnificent, meaningless enthusiasms, and splendid, blind generosities ; a world with a welcome for everything but reality, and tolerance for everything but plain, hard thinking—the world of Heartbreak Bus.

CHAPTER VIII

It will be clear now why Life Force worshippers are in difficulties, and why some of them are deserting science and others are trying to twist reality into shapes which will suit their brand of modern religion or mathematics. They have various ways of dealing with the contradictions and confusions which came into the open when they turned their backs on Kelvin, but none has dealt with the problem so simply as Shaw. He adopts shock tactics which have so far dumbfounded his opponents. He doesn't dodge the contradictions ; he accepts them, and is not in the least afraid to contradict himself in public. It is on just this point that his followers chide him, and say peevishly that he is deserting them when they are really deserting him. They agree to bow down to Irrational Power, and yet they baulk at the first inconsistency they meet. Inconsistencies are really Life Force trade marks, and the bold way in which they show up in Shaw's work must delight the heart of any reasonable man. They are like the anomalies in a really good detective story— they all check out in the end against the central anomaly. The Napoleon scene in *Back to Methuselah* and the Epilogue in *St. Joan*, and such other pieces of anti-climax are essential to the plays that contain them. The Life Force philosophy reduces every situation to absurdity, and Shaw has to abandon argument and let the characters behave wildly so that under cover of farce he may get back to sanity. Minor absurdities are required to balance the main absurdity. Millions take shelter from facts behind the comfortable-looking belief in eternal evolution, and then sheepishly refuse to recognise the curious consequences in which they become involved. Shaw gathers the oddities to himself, and with innocent audacity makes play out of them. He hugs his contradictions and magically turns them into an international reputation for anti-climax.

He assumes that there is no truth and then spends his life hunting for it. He teaches that institutions cramp the human spirit, and then tries to build up institutions which will free it. He says God doesn't yet exist and then sends out a Black Girl to search for him. He says that his religion is based on science and then disowns science. He says he has found the true religion and says that there is no true religion. Why, only the other day, in a Broadcast to Schools, he scoffed at the precept that men should love their enemies and the next minute he was advising the pupils to treat those they disliked as they would their best friends (*The Listener*, June 23rd, 1937).

It is these clashes with himself that provoke people into writing books about him and his views. Mrs.

Le Mesurier was so exasperated by *The Intelligent Woman's Guide to Socialism* that she sat down and wrote *The Socialist Woman's Guide to Intelligence*. She says :

> His book has provoked me past silence. I have put before my readers as clearly as I could some of the flaws, fallacies and inconsistencies with which it seems to me to bristle. It is amazing that even an ordinarily clever man, much less one with a super-brain like Mr. Shaw's, should have perpetrated seriously some of the remarks he has allowed himself to make.

She should have remembered his own warning that " even the cleverest man will believe what he wishes to believe, in spite of all the facts and all the textbooks in the world."

She spends 200 pages in showing up his various changes of front, with scrupulous quotation and reference, but in the end she seems to grow weary of the hopelessness of her task :

> If the book is picked up at random and a few pages read here and there, it makes stimulating and provocative reading. But when a serious attempt is made to follow a consistent argument from one chapter to another, the trail is blurred and all seems vague and confused. . . . Mr. Shaw leaps from theme to theme with bewildering rapidity, and one is left baffled, as after watching the zigzag path of flashes of

lightning across a dark sky, with an impression
of dazzling brilliance but no sense of direction.
. . . One thing is certain, and that is, that
whatever has been written about the book here
or elsewhere, is, in a sense, bound to be wrong !
Because, however accurately Mr. Shaw may
have been quoted and summarised, an indus-
trious reader is sure to be able to delve into
some recess of this mine of words and discover
that he has also said something quite different.

Then listen to Mr. John Strachey in the *Spectator*,
November 6th, 1936 :

Mr. Shaw is wrong. He is wrong, not
because he disagrees with me, but because he
disagrees with every other instructed Socialist
and Communist who has ever written on the
subject. Of course, Mr. Shaw was at liberty
to redefine the words in a new sense, if he had
explained that this was what he was doing.
But he has never done this, and has thus caused
very considerable confusion.

Or take Father Leslie Walker, S.J. He has been
reading *The Adventures of the Black Girl in her Search
for God*, and Shaw's jumpiness about words bothers
him. He finds that " science," for instance, has two
meanings :

science $_1$ = a spring of purest water.

science $_2$ = a source polluted and dangerous.

and, like Mrs. Le Mesurier, he is a little dazed to
find an eminent man contradicting himself with such

199

energy.   He is puzzled and as he says in his Prologue
to *The Return to God* :

> It is in part because I am puzzled that
> I am going to write this book. I am sceptical
> about the fresh-water supply because, in the
> course of his "Adventures," Mr. Shaw seems to
> have done not a little to poison the wells of
> Science from which he would have me draw.

He finds that Shaw is facing both ways, and he
seems to think the position unnatural. But what
other position is possible for Life Force prophets ?
They must always be travelling north and south,
always setting out as they are arriving, always
gazing at their own backs as they progress round and
round the fatal enclosure :

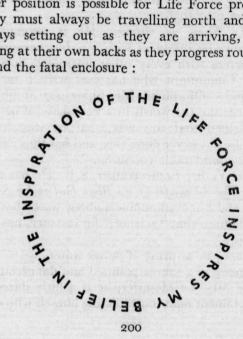

OF THE LIFE FORCE INSPIRES MY BELIEF IN THE INSPIRATION

Shaw's contradictions turn about everything, but mainly about Christianity and sex. He is for ever dealing with them, for ever turning them upside down and inside out—searching. He seems to say at once about each that it is the only thing worth considering, and that it is an absurdity ; he wants them and he wants them wiped out ; they are simultaneously good and evil. A mother with her baby is the most important thing in the world, and love is an illusion to be laughed off the face of the earth : " When we want to read of the deeds that are done for love, whither do we turn ? To the murder column ; and there we are rarely disappointed " (*Prefaces*, p. 715).

Contradictory urges make him careless. Or rather—for he is never careless—they dull his vision. There is no man more scrupulous for the integrity of the written word, yet when he wishes to show that Christ and St. Paul were at odds with one another about marriage, he suddenly begins to read the Bible so blindly that he attributes St. Paul's statements (1 Cor. vii) to Jesus, and thus makes his argument bite its own head off (*Prefaces*, p. 561). Then, again, when he wants to scoff at love, he looks to La Rochefoucauld for support, and quotes him as saying : " very few people would ever imagine themselves in love if they had never read anything about it " (*Prefaces*, p. 108), and is so pleased with the misquotation that he stores it away and repeats seven years later : " Love did nothing but prove the

201

soundness of La Rochefoucauld's saying that very few people would fall in love if they never read anything about it " (*Prefaces*, p. 380). O blind and perverse ! How could anyone believe for a minute that a Frenchman would say anything so idiotic, and how did Shaw come to offer such strange and heavy-handed renderings of the delicious " Il y a des gens qui n'auroient jamais été amoureux s'ils n'avoient jamais entendu parler de l'amour ? "

The treatment of love in *The Adventures of the Black Girl* is even stranger and more perverse. On p. 7 the woman missionary is described as an odd little body who :

> had settled down in the African forest to teach little African children to love$_1$ Christ and adore the Cross. She was a born apostle of love$_2$. At school she had adored one or other of her teachers with an idolatry that was proof against all snubbing, but had never cared much for girls of her own age and standing. At eighteen she began falling in love$_3$ with earnest clergymen, and actually became engaged to six of them in succession. But when it came to the point, she always broke it off; for these love$_4$ affairs, full at first of ecstatic happiness and hope, somehow became unreal and eluded her in the end. The clergymen, thus suddenly and unaccountably disengaged, did not always conceal their sense of relief and escape, as if they too had discovered that the dream was only a

dream, or a sort of metaphor by which they
had striven to express the real thing, but not
itself the real thing.

One of the jilted, however, committed
suicide ; and this tragedy gave her an extraordinary joy. It seemed to take her from a
fool's paradise of false happiness into a real
region in which intense suffering became
transcendent rapture.

Here are the clues for this crazy cross-word puzzle :

$Love_1$ = Charity.
$Love_2$ = 1, 3 or 4.
$Love_3$ = Sentimentalising.
$Love_4$ = Perverted.

It is a strange, frothy, clever, repellent opening, and
it seems to have little to do with what follows. But
when Christ is brought on the scene it will be found
that the motif is repeated and developed. On p. 29
the Black Girl meets " the conjuror," who is repre-
sented as a feeble, well-meaning, touchy, ricky-ticky-
tavy young man. The Black Girl, full up with
Man and Superman, hardly gives him a chance to get
in a word edgeways :

" I've seen worse kings," said the black girl,
" so you need not blush. Well, let you be
King Solomon, and let me be the Queen of
Sheba, same as in the Bible. I come to you
and say that I love you. That means I have
come to take possession of you. I come with

the love of a lioness and eat you up, and make you a part of myself. From this time, you will have to think, not of what pleases you, but of what pleases me. I will stand between you and yourself, between you and God. Is not that a terrible tyranny? Love is a devouring thing. Can you imagine heaven with love in it?"

"In my heaven there is nothing else. What else is heaven but love?" said the conjuror boldly but uncomfortably.

"It is glory. It is the home of God and his thoughts; there is no billing and cooing there, no clinging to one another like a tick to a sheep. The missionary, my teacher, talks of love; but she has run away from all her lovers to do God's work. The whites turn their eyes away from me lest they should love me. There are companies of men and women who have devoted themselves to God's work, but though they call themselves brotherhoods and sisterhoods, they do not speak to one another."

It all gives the curious fleeting impression of love being pursued by distortion and hatred, and yet there is also in it that equally curious redeeming childish quality which persists through all Shaw's writings. "There's 'glory' for you," says he, just like Humpty-Dumpty:

"But 'glory' doesn't mean, 'a nice knock-down argument,'" Alice objected.

"When *I* use a word," Humpty Dumpty

said in rather a scornful tone, " it means just what I choose it to mean, neither more nor less."

" The question is," said Alice, " whether you *can* make words mean so many different things. "

Shaw himself was apparently rather puzzled by the *Adventures of the Black Girl*. He tells his readers on p. 59 that he was inspired to write it—that he was, in fact, only a penholder—and he warns them that it may be all nonsense :

I know by observation and introspection that the instrument on which the inspiring force plays may be a very faulty one, and may even end like Bunyan in The Holy War, by making the most ridiculous nonsense of his message.

But he seems to have no doubt that it is the wish of the Life Force that belief and trust in Christ be wiped out so that the modern State may come into its own, for his last words on p. 74 are :

When the question of the existence of Noah's idol is raised on the point, vital to high civilisation, whether our children shall continue to be brought up to worship it and compound for their sins by sacrificing to it, or, more cheaply, by sheltering themselves behind another's sacrifice to it, then whoever hesitates to bring down the knobkerry with might and main is ludicrously unfit to have any part in the government of a modern State. The importance of a

message to that effect at the present world
crisis is probably at the bottom of my curious
and sudden inspiration to write this tale
instead of cumbering theatrical literature with
another stage comedy.

This nightmare view of Christian belief may
offend the orthodox, but they must remember that
Shaw has been working all his life on inside information about Christianity gathered prior to 1866, and
that his doctrinal age is probably about nine years.
The Sunday-school teaching of that period appears to
have been very crude—he was taught, for instance,
that all Catholics would sizzle in hell—and it is
evident from the *Adventures* that many early misconceptions were still flourishing in 1932.

It will be hard for many to believe that the author
of *St. Joan* remained all his life so immature and
uninformed about the essentials of Christian doctrine
—but it is a fact—or rather it is an hypothesis which
fits the facts. This does not mean that it will fit
all the Shaws. For this book is not an attempt to
dissect a real man, but an effort to find some key
to a set of writings. It makes no pretence to offer
a picture of the real Shaw, still less explain him.
A botanist doesn't explain a tree—in fact, when he
is finished with the root and the sap and the leaves,
there is precious little tree left. Still, the leaves are
interesting and have a story to tell. Shaw's works
must stand by themselves if they are to stand at all,
and whatever pitfalls lie in the way of an attempt to

see them and their writer as they may be seen in
A.D. 2000, or even A.D. 2,000,000, must be gaily faced.
Let there be no bones about this either ; let nothing
be lacking that can add to the defiance of this
challenge—of belief in a perfectly reliable GOD and
eternal order—to the Shavian creed of eternal confusion, with its morality perpetually in the melting-
pot. All that matters, in what is written here, might
be written any time by anyone with a set of Shaw's
works, a few standard history books, a real world,
and some common sense, at his disposal. There is
no appeal to anything but the evidence which they
offer, and there is no need to turn back when the
evidence piles up overwhelmingly to show that those
works were produced by a man behind whose beard
and bushy eyebrows a child was hiding.

There is a flesh-and-blood Shaw who goes about
the world radiating such bracing kindliness that the
magazines and newspapers teem with the pleasant,
if rather puzzled, references of those who have made
personal contact with him. Whether the Shaw who
wrote the books is the same Shaw or not, does not
matter here ; the whole point is, that they were
written by two different persons. It is convenient—
saving their presence—to call them George and
Bernard, and to visualise one of them as a prophet-
at-a-loss, rather ignored by the general public (who
ever heard of George Shaw ?) and to think of the other
as that Peter Pan, that eternal youth, that popular
favourite whose name is a household word.

When these two are at work together, it is very trying. In the second act of *Heartbreak House* they pose, for a few pages, as Captain Shotover and Ellie. To make it hard, Bernard is dressed up as " an ancient but still hardy man with an immense white beard, in a reefer jacket," but he has " a whistle hanging from his neck," which is just right. George comes on demurely as " a pretty girl, slender, fair, and intelligent looking." To make matters worse, they are inclined to swop places as that earnest dialogue proceeds. It is all rather hard on people who are going to the theatre for a night's relaxation ; but after all, isn't there the burglar and Mrs. Hushabye, and the rum-drinking—oh, there's lots of drollery in that play.

Bernard has wonderful vision ; he is a natural observer who gathers material as he goes, and hands it to George to sort out. In a way this is hard on George, for he hasn't the head for such a job ; but he is a great worker, and, under Life Force management, he has arranged the material so that Creative Evolution may be staged as the religion of the twentieth century. The curious thing is that Bernard sometimes comes out in front to take a look at George's God and says that he doesn't think much of either of them. He and Ann agreed that George was just " Talking "—talking through his hat—that time he got himself up as Jack Tanner.

Another way of putting all this is to say that George does not think in abstract terms. Instead of a sequence of thought, he offers a series of vivid pictures, each with a high emotional content and something in common with the one which went before it. He starts off with his conclusion and then goes on in lively fashion to personal applications and particular instances, all bearing progressively on what he wants his readers to believe. The selection is kaleidoscopic and the presentation marvellous; it is word pageantry as gorgeous as a royal procession, and as hypnotic. It makes some people worshipful, others wild, and a few a little impatient that a man should take so long to grow up. The process is applied to all topics like a formula, and shows little change with passing years :

1903 :

But ordinary men cannot produce really impressive art-works. Those who can are men of genius : that is, men selected by Nature to carry on the work of building up an intellectual consciousness of her own instinctive purpose. Accordingly, we observe in the man of genius all the unscrupulousness and all the " self-sacrifice " (the two things are the same) of Woman. He will risk the stake and the cross , starve, when necessary, in a garret all his life ; study women and live on their work and care as Darwin studied worms and lived upon sheep ; work his nerves into rags without payment, a sublime altruist in his disregard of himself, an atrocious egoist in his disregard of others. Here

Woman meets a purpose as impersonal and irresistible as her own ; and the clash is sometimes tragic. (*Prefaces*, p. 157.)

1908 :

There is no subject on which more dangerous nonsense is talked and thought than marriage. If the mischief stopped at talking and thinking it would be bad enough ; but it goes further into disastrous anarchical action. Because our marriage law is inhuman and unreasonable to the point of downright abomination, the bolder and more rebellious spirits form illicit unions, defiantly sending cards round to their friends announcing what they have done. Young women come to me and ask me whether I think they ought to consent to marry the man they have decided to live with ; and they are perplexed and astonished when I, who am supposed (heaven knows why !) to have the most advanced views attainable on the subject, urge them on no account to compromise themselves without the security of an authentic wedding ring. (*Prefaces*, p. 1.)

1910 :

Childhood is a stage in the process of that continual remanufacture of the Life Stuff by which the human race is perpetuated. The Life Force either will not or cannot achieve immortality except in very low organisms : indeed it is by no means ascertained that even the amœba is immortal. Human beings visibly wear out, though they last longer than their friends the dogs. Turtles, parrots, and elephants are believed to be capable of outliving the memory of the oldest human inhabitant. But the fact that new ones are born conclusively proves that they are not immortal. (*Prefaces*, p. 45.)

1916 :

Setting aside the huge mass of inculcated Christ-worship which has no real significance because it has no intelligence, there is, among people who are really free to think for themselves on the subject, a great deal of hearty dislike of Jesus and of contempt for his failure to save himself and overcome his enemies by personal bravery and cunning as Mahomet did. I have heard this feeling expressed far more impatiently by persons brought up in England as Christians than by Mahometans, who are, like their prophet, very civil to Jesus, and allow him a place in their esteem and veneration at least as high as we accord to John the Baptist. (*Prefaces*, p. 526.)

Let us be clear about the meaning of the terms. A genius is a person, who, seeing farther and probing deeper than other people, has a different set of ethical valuations from theirs, and has energy enough to give effect to this extra vision and its valuations in whatever manner best suits his or her specific talents.

A saint is one who having practised heroic virtues, and enjoyed revelations or powers which the Church classes technically as supernatural, is eligible for canonisation. If a historian is Anti-Feminist, and does not believe women to be capable of genius in the traditional masculine departments, he will never make anything of Joan, whose genius was turned to practical account mainly in soldiering and politics. (*Prefaces*, p. 584.)

1933 :

All modern progressive and revolutionary movements are at bottom attacks on private property. A Chancellor of the Exchequer apologising for an increase in the surtax, a Fascist dictator organising a Corporate State, a Soviet Commissar ejecting a kulak and adding his acres to a collective farm, are all running the same race, though all of them except the Commissar may be extremely reluctant to win it. For in the long run the power to exterminate is too grave to be left in any hands but those of a thoroughly Communist Government responsible to the whole community. The landlord with his writ of ejectment and the employer with his sack must finally go the way of the nobleman with his sword and his benefit of clergy, and of Hannibal Chollop with his bowie knife and pistol. (*Prefaces*, p. 355.)

Some people, like Mrs. Le Mesurier, Mr. Strachey, and Father Walker, hold that thinking should be done with the intellect, but these passages and thousands of others like them show what colourful work can be done by the emotions. Shaw's thought is the swift-flowing, impulsive imagery-thinking of a child. The Fabian Essay on Rent is full of it. It is a shocking thing to have to say, but it really must be said—Shaw does not understand economic science. He knows all about rent. Two hundred years of Kilkenny, topped off with four years of a Molesworth Street estate office, taught him the way of a man with land. He got his theories of value from books, but he learnt landlordism in a practical school. In nineteenth-century England, land-lordism and the structure of society were so closely linked that it was easy to mistake one for the other. It was natural for Shaw, pursuing his empirical way, to see everything in terms of rent, and to ignore the credit system ; for rent comes in chunks that can be counted, whereas credit is an intangible element too evasive for pictorial methods of thinking ; it is like value which also evaded him as it dived frantically into a maze of differentials ; but what he loses on the calculus he makes up in careful observation among the common swings and roundabouts. Just when George's incompetent theorising threatens to have serious consequences, Bernard comes along and puts in a brass tack.

Neither of them understands economic science.

But is there such a science, and do the economists
themselves understand it ? All engineers agree on
fundamental questions like " What is a horse-power,
and how does it exchange for calories ? " and so
they can get ahead ; but the economists have not
yet decided the question : " What is a man's soul
and how much is it worth ? " Some of them
are haggling over it, and some cannot even see that
the science of economics does not emerge till that
value is fixed in hard cash, or commodities, or at
least in terms of a printed card. The Marxians agree
that the answer is all in terms of material needs and
satisfactions ; and so long as that answer holds, their
science will hold. If man consents to enslavement,
problems of value vanish and economics becomes a
stable science with firm unchanging laws. George,
whose taste runs rather to libraries, uses the
Marxian answer as a foundation stone, but Bernard
makes all his Communistic friends uneasy by throwing back his young head and laughing at it.

It is perfectly clear that each of them is trying
hard to be faithful to his tutors. They had no
ordinary education : George was brought up by the
Kilkenny Shaws and John Vandaleur Lee, till he
got into the hands of Helmholtz, Tyndall, Rousseau
and Marx ; Bernard started with his mother and
an Irish Catholic nurse, and then went on to Mozart,
Shakespeare, Michael Angelo and Dickens ; both
of them sat at the feet of Shelley and Wagner.
How can any of us compete with such a combina-

tion ? We can only watch it competing with itself in that conflict called his works, that record of his researches which is such a complete guide to the process by which the idea of Propagation of Species, made dogma, leads men (even men like Marx and Buckle and Freud) into the darkness and enchains their minds.

George is a slave. He bows down to that dogma and adores before the Life Force ; he works for it, or perhaps it would be truer to say it works through him. Listen to his surrender :

I PERCEIVE THE VALUE AND TRUTH OF CALVIN'S CONVICTION THAT ONCE A MAN IS BORN, IT IS TOO LATE TO SAVE HIM OR DAMN HIM ; YOU MAY "EDUCATE" HIM AND "FORM HIS CHARACTER" UNTIL YOU ARE BLACK IN THE FACE ; HE IS PREDESTINATE AND HIS SOUL CANNOT BE CHANGED ANY MORE THAN A SILK PURSE CAN BE CHANGED INTO A SOW'S EAR. (August, 1909, *Pen Portraits and Reviews*, p. 91.)

This is the burden of his message and the core of his teaching. The Life Force surges blindly, tapping out its slaves by the million : tap tap . . Rich man, Poor man . . tap tap tap . . . Tinker, Tailor, Thief . . . tap tap tap tap. . . . Sinner, Saint, Hero, Hussy . . . . and so *ad infinitum*.

Bernard is free. He values the gift of freedom and power of choice above all things and rejects that accursed doctrine. It has tried in a hundred disguises over nearly as many years to entrap him, but he always eludes it. It presents itself as the garb of maturity, but if the acceptance of THAT is the price of growing up, he prefers to remain free and a child for ever. This is why he had led George such a dance ; this is why he has so annoyed and bewildered his votaries ; this is why all the rest of us love him.

ACKNOWLEDGMENTS

I am deeply indebted to the following books :

Candlelight Attic, by Cecily Hallack.
St. Catherine, by Alice Curtayne.
Plays and Prefaces, by Bernard Shaw.
Shaw, Playboy and Prophet, by Archibald Henderson.
Progress and Religion, by Christopher Dawson.
The Nature of Belief, by U. C. D'Arcy, S.J.

and also to Father Stephen Brown, S.J., to Father Aegidius Dovlan, O.P., and to Mr. F. J. Sheed.

J. P. HACKETT.

Dublin, July 1937